Terrorism and Violence

Terrorism and Violence

Jabbar Hussain

Saurabh
Publishing House
4263/3, Ansari Road,
Darya Ganj, New Delhi-110002

Published by:
SAURABH PUBLISHING HOUSE

Distributed by:
LOTUS PRESS
4263/3, Ansari Road, Darya Ganj, New Delhi-110002
Ph.: 32903912, 23280047 • E-mail : lotus_press@sify.com

Saurabh Publishing is an imprint of
Lotus Press

Terrorism and Violence

ISBN : 978-81-89005-48-1 (H/B)

Printed in India by Anand Sons, Delhi

Preface

The definition of terrorism has proved controversial. Various legal systems and government agencies use different definitions of terrorism in their national legislation. Moreover, the International community has been slow to formulate a universally agreed, legally binding definition of this crime. These difficulties arise from the fact that the term "terrorism" is politically and emotionally charged. In this regard, Angus Martyn, briefing the Australian Parliament, stated that "The international community has never succeeded in developing an accepted comprehensive definition of terrorism. During the 1970s and 1980s, the United Nations attempts to define the term foundered mainly due to differences of opinion between various members about the use of violence in the context of conflicts over national liberation and self-determination." These divergences have made it impossible for the United Nations to conclude a Comprehensive Convention on International Terrorism that incorporates a single, all-encompassing, legally binding, criminal law definition terrorism. Nonetheless, the international community has adopted a series of sectoral conventions that define and criminalize various types of terrorist activities.

Moreover, since 1994, the United Nations General Assembly has repeatedly condemned terrorist acts using the following political description of terrorism: "Criminal acts intended or calculated to provoke a state of terror in the general public, a group of persons or particular persons for political purposes are in any circumstance unjustifiable, whatever the considerations of a political, philosophical, ideological, racial, ethnic, religious or any other nature that may be invoked to justify them."

The major topics dealt in this book are: *Introduction to Terrorism; History of Terrorism; Terrorism and Behaviour; Terrorism: A Modern Scourge; State Terrorism and Comprehensive Conventions; Terrorism in India; Insurgency in Jammu and Kashmir; Khalistan Movement and Sikh Extremism; Insurgency in Northeast India and Naxalite Movement; Unified Communist Party of Nepal; Pakistan and State Terrorism; Gujarat Violence; Anti-Christian and Violence in India; etc.*

We express our gratitude to various scholars, teachers and friends for their assistance and guidance. Finally, we thank our publisher for bringing out this book in very limited time.

–Author

Contents

1
Introduction to Terrorism

Terrorism is the systematic use of terror especially as a means of coercion. At present, the International community has been unable to formulate a universally agreed, legally binding, criminal law definition of terrorism. Common definitions of terrorism refer only to those violent acts which are intended to create fear (terror), are perpetrated for an ideological goal and deliberately target or disregard the safety of non-combatants (civilians).

Some definitions also include acts of unlawful violence and war. The history of terrorist organizations suggests that they do not select terrorism for its political effectiveness. Individual terrorists tend to be motivated more by a desire for social solidarity with other members of their organisation than by political platforms or strategic objectives, which are often murky and undefined.

The word "terrorism" is politically and emotionally charged and this greatly compounds the difficulty of providing a precise definition. Studies have found over 100 definitions of "terrorism". The concept of terrorism may itself be controversial as it is often used by state authorities to delegitimize political or other opponents and potentially legitimize the state's own use of armed force against opponents (such use of force may itself be described as "terror" by opponents of the state).

Terrorism has been practiced by a broad array of political organisations for furthering their objectives. It has been practiced by both right-wing and left-wing political parties, nationalistic groups, religious groups, revolutionaries and ruling governments. One form is the use of violence against noncombatants for the purpose of gaining publicity for a group, cause, or individual.

"Terror" comes from a Latin *terrere* meaning "to frighten". The *terror cimbricus* was a panic and state of emergency in Rome in response to the approach of warriors of the Cimbri tribe in 105 BC. The Jacobins cited this precedent when imposing a Reign of Terror during the French Revolution. After the Jacobins lost power, the word "terrorist" became a term of abuse. Although the Reign of Terror was imposed by a government, in modern times "terrorism" usually refers to the killing of innocent people by a private group in such a way as to create a media spectacle. This meaning can be traced back to Sergey Nechayev, who described himself as a "terrorist". Nechayev founded the Russian terrorist group "People's Retribution" in 1869.

In November 2004, a United Nations Secretary General's report described terrorism as any act "intended to cause death or serious bodily harm to civilians or non-combatants with the purpose of intimidating a population or compelling a government or an international organisation to do or abstain from doing any act".

Definition

The definition of terrorism has proved controversial. Various legal systems and government agencies use different definitions of terrorism in their national legislation. Moreover, the International community has been slow to formulate a universally agreed, legally binding definition of this crime. These difficulties arise from the fact that the term "terrorism" is politically and emotionally charged. In this regard, Angus Martyn, briefing the Australian Parliament, stated that "The international community has never succeeded in developing an accepted comprehensive definition of terrorism. During the 1970s and 1980s, the United Nations attempts to define the term foundered mainly due to differences of opinion between various members about the use of violence in the context of conflicts over national liberation and self-determination." These divergences have made it impossible for the United Nations to conclude a Comprehensive Convention on International Terrorism that incorporates a single, all-encompassing, legally binding, criminal law definition terrorism. Nonetheless, the international community has adopted a series of sectoral conventions that define and criminalize various types of terrorist activities. Moreover, since 1994, the United Nations General Assembly has repeatedly condemned terrorist acts using the following political description of terrorism: "Criminal acts intended or calculated to provoke a state of terror in the general public, a group of persons or particular persons for political purposes are in any circumstance unjustifiable, whatever the considerations of a political, philosophical, ideological, racial, ethnic, religious or any other nature that may be invoked to justify them."

Bruce Hoffman, a well-known scholar, has noted that:

It is not only individual agencies within the same governmental apparatus that cannot agree on a single definition of terrorism. Experts and other long-established scholars in the field are equally incapable of reaching a consensus. In the first edition of his magisterial survey, "Political terrorism: A Research Guide,"

Alex Schmid devoted more than a hundred pages to examining more than a hundred different definition of terrorism in a effort to discover a broadly acceptable, reasonably comprehensive explication of the word. Four years and a second edition later, Schimd was no closer to the goal of his quest, conceding in the first sentence of the revised volume that the "search for an adequate definition is still on"

Walter Laqueur despaired of defining terrorism in both editions of his monumental work on the subject, maintaining that it is neither possible to do so nor worthwhile to make the attempt."

Nonetheless, Hoffman himself believes it is possible to identify some key characteristics of terrorism.

By distinguishing terrorists from other types of criminals and terrorism from other forms of crime, we come to appreciate that terrorism is:

- ineluctably political in aims and motives
- violent – or, equally important, threatens violence
- designed to have far-reaching psychological repercussions beyond the immediate victim or target
- conducted by an organization with an identifiable chain of command or conspiratorial cell structure (whose members wear no uniform or identifying insignia) and
- perpetrated by a subnational group or non-state entity.

A definition proposed by Carsten Bockstette at the George C. Marshall Center for European Security Studies, underlines the psychological and tactical aspects of terrorism:

> *"Terrorism is defined as political violence in an asymmetrical conflict that is designed to induce terror and psychic fear (sometimes indiscriminate) through the violent victimization and destruction of noncombatant targets (sometimes iconic symbols). Such acts are meant to send a message from an illicit clandestine organisation. The purpose of terrorism is to exploit the media in order to achieve maximum attainable publicity as an amplifying force multiplier in order to influence the targeted audience(s) in order to reach short- and midterm political goals and/or desired long-term end states."*

Walter Laqueur, of the Center for Strategic and International Studies, noted that "the only general characteristic of terrorism generally agreed upon is that terrorism involves violence and the threat of violence". This criterion alone does not produce, however, a useful definition, since it includes many violent acts not usually considered terrorism: war, riot, organised crime, or even a simple assault. Property destruction that does not endanger life is not usually considered a violent crime, but some have described property destruction by the Earth Liberation Front and Animal Liberation Front as violence and terrorism; see eco-terrorism.

Terrorist attacks are usually carried out in such a way as to maximize the severity and length of the psychological impact. Each act of terrorism is a "performance" devised to have an impact on many large audiences. Terrorists also attack national symbols, to show power and to attempt to shake the foundation of the country or society they are opposed to. This may negatively affect a government, while increasing the prestige of the given terrorist organization and/or ideology behind a terrorist act.

Terrorist acts frequently have a political purpose. Terrorism is a political tactic, like letter-writing or protesting, which is used by activists when they believe that no other means will effect the kind of change they desire. The change is desired so badly that failure to achieve change is seen as a worse outcome than the deaths of civilians. This is often where the inter-relationship between terrorism and religion occurs. When a political struggle is integrated into the framework of a religious or "cosmic" struggle, such as over the control of an ancestral homeland or holy site such as Israel and Jerusalem, failing in the political goal (nationalism) becomes equated with spiritual failure, which, for the highly committed, is worse than their own death or the deaths of innocent civilians.

Very often, the victims of terrorism are targeted not because they are threats, but because they are specific "symbols, tools, animals or corrupt beings" that tie into a specific view of the world that the terrorists possess. Their suffering accomplishes the terrorists' goals of instilling fear, getting their message out to an audience or otherwise satisfying the demands of their often radical religious and political agendas.

Some official, governmental definitions of terrorism use the criterion of the illegitimacy or unlawfulness of the act. To distinguish between actions authorized by a government (and thus "lawful") and those of other actors, including individuals and small groups. Using this criterion, actions that would otherwise qualify as terrorism would not be considered terrorism if they were government sanctioned. For example, firebombing a city, which is designed to affect civilian support for a cause, would not be considered terrorism if it were authorized by a government. This criterion is inherently problematic and is not universally accepted, because: it denies the existence of state terrorism; the same act may or may not be classed as terrorism depending on whether its sponsorship is traced to a "legitimate" government; "legitimacy" and "lawfulness" are subjective, depending on the perspective of one government or another and it diverges from the historically accepted meaning and origin of the term.

Among the various definitions there are several that do not recognize the possibility of legitimate use of violence by civilians against an invader in an occupied country. Other definitions would label as terrorist groups only the resistance movements that oppose an invader with violent acts that undiscriminately kill or harm civilians and non-combatants, thus making a distinction between lawful and unlawful use of violence. According to Ali Khan, the distinction lies ultimatedly in a political judgement.

An associated and arguably more easily definable, but *not equivalent* term is violent non-state actor. The semantic scope of this term includes not only "terrorists", but while excluding some individuals or groups who have previously been described as "terrorists" and also explicitly excludes state terrorism.

Pejorative Use

The terms "terrorism" and "terrorist" (someone who engages in terrorism) carry strong negative connotations. These terms are often used as political labels, to condemn violence or the threat of violence by certain actors as immoral, indiscriminate, unjustified or to condemn an entire segment of a population. Those labelled "terrorists" by their opponents rarely identify themselves as such and typically use other terms or terms specific to their situation, such as separatist, freedom fighter, liberator, revolutionary, vigilante, militant, paramilitary, guerrilla, rebel, patriot, or any similar-meaning word in other languages and cultures. Jihadi, mujahiddin and fedayeen are similar Arabic words which have entered the English lexicon. It is common for both parties to a conflict to describe each other as terrorists.

On the question of whether particular terrorist acts, such as killing civilians, can be justified as the lesser evil in a particular circumstance, philosophers have expressed different views: while, according to David Rodin, utilitarian philosophers can (in theory) conceive of cases in which the evil of terrorism is outweighed by the good which could not be achieved in a less morally costly way, in practice the "harmful effects of undermining the convention of non-combatant immunity is thought to outweigh the goods that may be achieved by particular acts of terrorism". Among the non-utilitarian philosophers, Michael Walzer argued that terrorism can be morally justified in only one specific case: when "a nation or community faces the extreme threat of complete destruction and the only way it can preserve itself is by intentionally targeting non-combatants, then it is morally entitled to do so".

In his book *Inside Terrorism* Bruce Hoffman offered an explanation of why the term *terrorism* becomes distorted:

> "On one point, at least, everyone agrees: *terrorism* is a pejorative term. It is a word with intrinsically negative connotations that is generally applied to one's enemies and opponents, or to those with whom one disagrees and would otherwise prefer to ignore. 'What is called terrorism,' Brian Jenkins has written, 'thus seems to depend on one's point of view. Use of the term implies a moral judgment and if one party can successfully attach the label *terrorist* to its opponent, then it has indirectly persuaded others to adopt its moral viewpoint.' Hence the decision to call someone or label some organisation *terrorist* becomes almost unavoidably subjective, depending largely on whether one sympathizes with or opposes the person/group/cause concerned. If one identifies with the victim of the violence, for example, then the act is terrorism. If, however, one identifies with the perpetrator, the violent act is regarded in a more sympathetic, if not positive (or, at the worst, an ambivalent) light and it is not terrorism."

The pejorative connotations of the word can be summed up in the aphorism, "One man's terrorist is another man's freedom fighter". This is exemplified when a group using irregular military methods is an ally of a state against a mutual enemy, but later falls out with the state and starts to use those methods against its former ally. During World War II, the Malayan People's Anti-Japanese Army was allied with the British, but during the Malayan Emergency, members of its successor (the Malayan Races Liberation Army), were branded "terrorists" by the British. More recently, Ronald

Reagan and others in the American administration frequently called the Afghan Mujahideen "freedom fighters" during their war against the Soviet Union, yet twenty years later, when a new generation of Afghan men are fighting against what they perceive to be a regime installed by foreign powers, their attacks are labelled "terrorism" by George W. Bush. Groups accused of terrorism understandably prefer terms reflecting legitimate military or ideological action. Leading terrorism researcher Professor Martin Rudner, director of the Canadian Centre of Intelligence and Security Studies at Ottawa's Carleton University, defines "terrorist acts" as attacks against civilians for political or other ideological goals and said:

> "There is the famous statement: 'One man's terrorist is another man's freedom fighter.' But that is grossly misleading. It assesses the validity of the cause when terrorism is an act. One can have a perfectly beautiful cause and yet if one commits terrorist acts, it is terrorism regardless."

Some groups, when involved in a "liberation" struggle, have been called "terrorists" by the Western governments or media. Later, these same persons, as leaders of the liberated nations, are called "statesmen" by similar organizations. Two examples of this phenomenon are the Nobel Peace Prize laureates Menachem Begin and Nelson Mandela.

Sometimes states which are close allies, for reasons of history, culture and politics, can disagree over whether or not members of a certain organisation are terrorists. For instance, for many years, some branches of the United States government refused to label members of the Irish Republican Army (IRA) as terrorists while the IRA was using methods against one of the United States' closest allies (Britain) which Britain branded as terrorism. This was highlighted by the Quinn *v.* Robinson case.

For these and other reasons, media outlets wishing to preserve a reputation for impartiality try to be careful in their use of the term.

Types of Terrorism

In early 1975, the Law Enforcement Assistant Administration in the United States formed the National Advisory Committee on Criminal Justice Standards and Goals. One of the five volumes that the committee wrote was entitled *Disorders and Terrorism,* produced by the Task Force on Disorders and Terrorism under the direction of H.H.A. Cooper, Director of the Task Force staff. The Task Force classified terrorism into six categories.

- **Civil disorder** – A form of collective violence interfering with the peace, security and normal functioning of the community.
- **Political terrorism** – Violent criminal behaviour designed primarily to generate fear in the community, or substantial segment of it, for political purposes.
- **Non-Political terrorism** – Terrorism that is not aimed at political purposes but which exhibits "conscious design to create and maintain a high degree of fear for coercive purposes, but the end is individual or collective gain rather than the achievement of a political objective."
- **Quasi-terrorism** – The activities incidental to the commission of crimes of violence that are similar in form and method to genuine terrorism but which nevertheless lack its essential ingredient. It is not the main purpose of the quasi-terrorists to induce terror in the immediate victim as in the case of genuine terrorism, but the quasi-terrorist uses the modalities and techniques of the genuine terrorist and produces similar consequences and reaction. For example, the

fleeing felon who takes hostages is a quasi-terrorist, whose methods are similar to those of the genuine terrorist but whose purposes are quite different.

- **Limited Political terrorism** – Genuine political terrorism is characterized by a revolutionary approach; limited political terrorism refers to "acts of terrorism which are committed for ideological or political motives but which are not part of a concerted campaign to capture control of the state.

- **Official or state terrorism** – "Referring to nations whose rule is based upon fear and oppression that reach similar to terrorism or such proportions." It may also be referred to as **Structural Terrorism** defined broadly as terrorist acts carried out by governments in pursuit of political objectives, often as part of their foreign policy.

Democracy and Domestic Terrorism

The relationship between domestic terrorism and democracy is very complex. Terrorism is most common in nations with intermediate political freedom and is least common in the most democratic nations. However, one study suggests that suicide terrorism may be an exception to this general rule. Evidence regarding this particular method of terrorism reveals that every modern suicide campaign has targeted a democracy–a state with a considerable degree of political freedom. The study suggests that concessions awarded to terrorists during the 1980s and 1990s for suicide attacks increased their frequency.

Some examples of "terrorism" in non-democracies include ETA in Spain under Francisco Franco, the Shining Path in Peru under Alberto Fujimori, the Kurdistan Workers Party when Turkey was ruled by military leaders and the ANC in South Africa. Democracies, such as the United Kingdom,

United States, Israel, Indonesia, India and the Philippines, have also experienced domestic terrorism.

While a democratic nation espousing civil liberties may claim a sense of higher moral ground than other regimes, an act of terrorism within such a state may cause a dilemma: whether to maintain its civil liberties and thus risk being perceived as ineffective in dealing with the problem; or alternatively to restrict its civil liberties and thus risk delegitimizing its claim of supporting civil liberties. This dilemma, some social theorists would conclude, may very well play into the initial plans of the acting terrorist(s); namely, to delegitimize the state.

Religious Terrorism

Religious terrorism is terrorism performed by groups or individuals, the motivation of which is typically rooted in the faith based tenets. Terrorist acts throughout the centuries have been performed on religious grounds with the hope to either spread or enforce a system of belief, viewpoint or opinion. Religious terrorism does not in itself necessarily define a specific religious standpoint or view, but instead usually defines an individual or a group view or interpretation of that belief system's teachings.

Perpetrators

The perpetrators of acts of terrorism can be individuals, groups, or states. According to some definitions, clandestine or semi-clandestine state actors may also carry out terrorist acts outside the framework of a state of war. However, the most common image of terrorism is that it is carried out by small and secretive cells, highly motivated to serve a particular cause and many of the most deadly operations in recent times, such as the September 11 attacks, the London underground bombing and the 2002 Bali bombing were planned and carried out by a close clique, composed of close friends, family members and other strong social networks. These groups benefited from the free flow of information and efficient telecommunications to succeed where others had failed.

Over the years, many people have attempted to come up with a terrorist profile to attempt to explain these individuals' actions through their psychology and social circumstances. Others, like Roderick Hindery, have sought to discern profiles in the propaganda tactics used by terrorists. Some security organizations designate these groups as *violent non-state actors*. A 2007 study by economist Alan B. Krueger found that terrorists were less likely to come from an impoverished background (28% *vs.* 33%) and more likely to have at least a high school education (47% *vs.* 38%). Another analysis found only 16% of terrorists came from impoverished families, *vs.* 30% of male Palestinians and over 60% had gone beyond high school, *vs.* 15% of the populace.

To avoid detection, a terrorist will look, dress and behave normally until executing the assigned mission. Some claim that attempts to profile terrorists based on personality, physical, or sociological traits are not useful. The physical and behavioral description of the terrorist could describe almost any normal person. However, the majority of terrorist attacks are carried out by military age men, aged 16–40.

State Sponsors

A state can sponsor terrorism by funding or harboring a terrorist organisation. Opinions as to which acts of violence by states consist of state-sponsored terrorism vary widely. When states provide funding for groups considered by some to be terrorist, they rarely acknowledge them as such.

State Terrorism

> "Civilization is based on a clearly defined and widely accepted yet often unarticulated hierarchy. Violence done

> by those higher on the hierarchy to those lower is nearly always invisible, that is, unnoticed. When it is noticed, it is fully rationalized. Violence done by those lower on the hierarchy to those higher is unthinkable and when it does occur is regarded with shock, horror and the fetishization of the victims."
>
> — Derrick Jensen

As with "terrorism" the concept of "state terrorism" is controversial. The Chairman of the United Nations Counter-Terrorism Committee has stated that the Committee was conscious of 12 international Conventions on the subject and none of them referred to State terrorism, which was not an international legal concept. If States abused their power, they should be judged against international conventions dealing with war crimes, international human rights and international humanitarian law. Former United Nations Secretary-General Kofi Annan has said that it is "time to set aside debates on so-called 'state terrorism'. The use of force by states is already thoroughly regulated under international law" However, he also made clear that, "regardless of the differences between governments on the question of definition of terrorism, what is clear and what we can all agree on is any deliberate attack on innocent civilians, regardless of one's cause, is unacceptable and fits into the definition of terrorism."

State terrorism has been used to refer to terrorist acts by governmental agents or forces. This involves the use of state resources employed by a state's foreign policies, such as using its military to directly perform acts of terrorism. Professor of Political Science Michael Stohl cites the examples that include Germany's bombing of London and the U.S. atomic destruction of Hiroshima during World War II. He argues that "the use of terror tactics is common in international relations and the state has been and remains a more likely employer of terrorism within the international system than insurgents." They also cite the First strike option as an example of the "terror of coercive diplomacy" as a form of this, which holds the world hostage with the implied threat of using nuclear weapons in "crisis management." They argue that the institutionalized form of terrorism has occurred as a result of changes that took place following World War II. In this analysis, state terrorism exhibited as a form of foreign policy was shaped by the presence and use of weapons of mass destruction and that the legitimizing of such violent behaviour led to an increasingly accepted form of this state behaviour.

State terrorism has also been used to describe peacetime actions by governmental agents such as the bombing of Pan Am Flight 103. Charles Stewart Parnell described William Ewart Gladstone's Irish Coercion Act as terrorism in his "no-Rent manifesto" in 1881, during the Irish Land War. The concept is also used to describe political repressions by governments against their own civilian population with the purpose to incite fear. For example, taking and executing civilian hostages or extrajudicial elimination campaigns are commonly considered "terror" or terrorism, for example, during the Red Terror or Great Terror. Such actions are often also described as democide or genocide which has been argued to be equivalent to state terrorism. Empirical studies on this have found that democracies have little democide.

Funding

State sponsors have constituted a major form of funding; for example, PLO, DFLP and some other terrorist groups were funded by the Soviet Union.

> "Revolutionary tax" is another major form of funding and essentially a euphemism for "protection money". Revolutionary taxes are typically extorted from businesses and they also "play a secondary role as one other means of intimidating the target population".

Other major sources of funding include kidnapping for ransoms, smuggling, fraud and robbery.

Tactics

Terrorism is a form of asymmetric warfare and is more common when direct conventional warfare won't be effective because forces vary greatly in power.

The context in which terrorist tactics are used is often a large-scale, unresolved political conflict. The type of conflict varies widely; historical examples include:

- Secession of a territory to form a new sovereign state
- Dominance of territory or resources by various ethnic groups
- Imposition of a particular form of government
- Economic deprivation of a population
- Opposition to a domestic government or occupying army
- Religious fanaticism

Terrorist attacks are often targeted to maximize fear and publicity, usually using explosives or poison. There is concern about terrorist attacks employing weapons of mass destruction. Terrorist organizations usually methodically plan attacks in advance and may train participants, plant undercover agents and raise money from supporters or through organized crime. Communications occur through modern telecommunications, or through old-fashioned methods such as couriers.

Responses

Responses to terrorism are broad in scope. They can include re-alignments of the political spectrum and reassessments of fundamental values.

Specific types of responses include:

- Targeted laws, criminal procedures, deportations and enhanced police powers
- Target hardening, such as locking doors or adding traffic barriers
- Preemptive or reactive military action
- Increased intelligence and surveillance activities
- Preemptive humanitarian activities
- More permissive interrogation and detention policies

The term **counter-terrorism** has a narrower connotation, implying that it is directed at terrorist actors.

Some 1,271 government organizations and 1,931 private companies work on programmes related to counterterrorism, homeland security and intelligence in about 10,000 locations across the United States.

Mass Media

Media exposure may be a primary goal of those carrying out terrorism, to expose issues that would otherwise be ignored by the media. Some consider this to be manipulation and exploitation of the media. Others consider terrorism itself to be a symptom of a highly controlled mass media, which does not otherwise give voice to alternative viewpoints, a view expressed by Paul Watson who has stated that controlled media is responsible for terrorism, because "you cannot get your information across any other way". Paul Watson's organisation Sea Shepherd has itself been branded "eco-terrorist", although it claims to have not caused any casualties.

The internet has created a new channel for groups to spread their messages. This has created a cycle of measures and counter measures by groups in support of and in opposition to terrorist movements. The United Nations has created its own online counter-terrorism resource.

The mass media will, on occasion, censor organizations involved in terrorism (through self-restraint or regulation) to discourage further terrorism. However, this may encourage organizations to perform more extreme acts of terrorism to be shown in the mass media. Conversely James F. Pastor explains the significant relationship between terrorism and the media and the underlying benefit each receives from the other.

There is always a point at which the terrorist ceases to manipulate the media gestalt. A point at which the violence may well escalate, but beyond which the terrorist has become symptomatic of the media gestalt itself. Terrorism as we ordinarily understand it is innately media-related.

—Novelist William Gibson

2
History of Terrorism

The history of terrorism is a history of well-known and historically significant individuals, entities and incidents associated, whether rightly or wrongly, with terrorism. Scholars agree that terrorism is a disputed term and very few of those labelled terrorists describe themselves as such.

Though many have been proposed, there is no consensus definition of the term "terrorism." This in part derives from the fact that the term is politically and emotionally charged, "a word with intrinsically negative connotations that is generally applied to one's enemies and opponents." Listed below are some of the historically important understandings of terror and terrorism and enacted but non-universal definitions of the term:

- **1795**. "Government intimidation during the Reign of Terror in France." The general sense of "systematic use of terror as a policy" was first recorded in English in 1798.
- **1916**. Gustave LeBon: "Terrorization has always been employed by revolutionaries no less than by kings, as a means of impressing their enemies and as an example to those who were doubtful about submitting to them . . ."
- **1937**. League of Nations convention language: "All criminal acts directed against a State and intended or calculated to create a state of terror in the minds of particular persons or a group of persons or the general public."

- **1987**. A definition proposed by Iran at an International Islamic Conference on Terrorism: "Terrorism is an act carried out to achieve an inhuman and corrupt *(mufsid)* objective and involving threat to security of any kind and violation of rights acknowledged by religion and mankind."

- **1988**. A proposed academic consensus definition: "Terrorism is an anxiety-inspiring method of repeated violent action, employed by (semi-) clandestine individual, group or state actors, for idiosyncratic, criminal or political reasons, whereby — in contrast to assassination — the direct targets of violence are not the main targets. The immediate human victims of violence are generally chosen randomly (targets of opportunity) or selectively (representative or symbolic targets) from a target population and serve as message generators."

- **1989**. United States: premeditated, politically motivated violence perpetrated against noncombatant targets by sub-national groups or clandestine agents.

- **1992**. A definition proposed by Alex P. Schmid to the United Nations Crime Branch: "Act of Terrorism = Peacetime Equivalent of War Crime."

- **2002**. European Union: ". . . given their nature or context, [acts which] may seriously damage a country or an international organisation where committed with the aim of seriously intimidating a population."

- **2003**. India: Referencing Schmid's 1992 proposal, the Supreme Court of India described terrorist acts as the "peacetime equivalents of war crimes."

- **2008**. Carsten Bockstette, a German military officer serving at the George C. Marshall Center for

European Security Studies, proposed the following definition: "political violence in an asymmetrical conflict that is designed to induce terror and psychic fear (sometimes indiscriminate) through the violent victimization and destruction of noncombatant targets (sometimes iconic symbols)."

Before the Reign of Terror

Scholars dispute whether the roots of terrorism date back to the first century and the Sicarii Zealots, to the eleventh century and the Al-Hashshashin, to the 19th century and Narodnaya Volya, or to other eras. The Sicarii and Hashshashin are described below, while the Narodnaya Volya is discussed in the 19th Century sub-section. Other pre-Reign of Terror historical events sometimes associated with terrorism are the Gunpowder Plot, an attempt to destroy the English Parliament in 1605 and the Boston Tea Party, an attack on British property by the Sons of Liberty in 1773, three years prior to the American Revolution.

In the 1st century CE, the Jewish Zealots in Iudaea Province rebelled, killing prominent collaborators with Roman rule. In 6 C.E., according to contemporary historian Josephus, Judas of Galilee formed a small and more extreme offshoot of the Zealots, the **Sicarii** ("dagger men"). Their efforts also directed against Jewish "collaborators," including temple priests, Sadducees, Herodians and other wealthy elites. According to Josephus, the Sicarii would hide short daggers under their cloaks, mingle with crowds at large festivals, murder their victims and then disappear into the panicked crowds. Their most successful assassination was of the high priest Jonathan.

In the late 11th century CE, the **Hashshashin** (a.k.a. the Assassins) arose, an offshoot of the Ismâ'îlî sect of Shia Muslims. Led by Hassan-i Sabbah and opposed to Fatimid rule, the Hashshashin militia seized Alamut and other fortress strongholds across Persia. Hashshashin forces were too small to challenge enemies militarily, so they assassinated city governors and military commanders in order to create alliances with militarily powerful neighbours. For example, they killed Janah al-Dawla, ruler of Homs, to please Ridwan of Aleppo and assassinated Mawdud, Seljuk Emir of Mosul, as a favour to the regent of Damascus. The Hashshashin also carried out assassinations as retribution. Under some definitions of terrorism, such assassinations do not qualify as terrorism, since killing a political leader does not intimidate political enemies or inspire revolt.

The Reign of Terror (1793-1794)

The Reign of Terror (September 5, 1793 – July 28, 1794) or simply The Terror (French: la Terreur) was a period of eleven months during the French Revolution when the ruling Jacobins employed violence, including mass executions by guillotine, in order to intimidate the regime's enemies and compel obedience to the state. The number killed totaled approximately 40,000 and among the guillotined were Louis XVI and Marie Antoinette. Putting an end to the Terror, on July 28, 1794, its most well known leader, Maximilien Robespierre, was guillotined by other members of France's ruling National Convention.

The Jacobins, most famously Robespierre, sometimes referred to themselves as "terrorists," and the word originated at that time.. Some modern scholars, however, do not consider the Reign of Terror a form of terrorism, in part because it was carried out by the French state.

19th Century

Terrorism was associated with the Reign of Terror in France until the mid-19th century, when the term began being associated with non-governmental groups. Anarchism, often in league with rising nationalism, was the most prominent ideology associated with terrorism. Attacks by various anarchist groups led to the assassination of a Russian Tsar and a U.S. President.

The 19th century saw the development of powerful, stable and affordable explosives and the gap closed between the firepower of the state and dissidents. Dynamite, in particular, inspired American and French anarchists and was central to their strategic thinking.

In mid-19th century Russia, many grew impatient with the slow pace of Tsarist reforms and anarchists such as Mikhail Bakunin maintained that progress was impossible without violence. Founded in 1878 and inspired by Bakunin and others, Narodnaya Volya used dynamite-packed bombs to kill Russian state officials in an effort to incite state retribution and mobilize the populace against the government. Inspired by Narodnaya Volya, several nationalist groups in the ailing Ottoman Empire began using violence against public figures in the 1890s, including the Hunchakian Revolutionary Party, the Armenian Revolutionary Federation and the Internal Macedonian Revolutionary Organization (IMRO).

The United States

Prior to the U.S. Civil War , **John Brown** (1800–1859) was an abolitionist who advocated and practiced armed opposition to slavery, leading several attacks between 1856 and 1859, the most famous in 1859 against the armory at Harpers Ferry. Local forces soon recaptured the fort and Brown, who was tried and executed for treason. A biographer of Brown has written that Brown's purpose was "to force the nation into a new political pattern by creating terror."

After the Civil War, on December 24, 1865, six Confederate veterans created the **Ku Klux Klan** (KKK). The KKK used violence, lynching, murder and acts of intimidation such as cross burning to oppress in particular African Americans and created a sensation with its masked forays' dramatic nature. The group's politics are generally perceived as white supremacy, anti-Semitism, racism, anti-Catholicism, homophobia and nativism. A KKK founder boasted that it was a nationwide organisation of 550,000 men and that it could muster 40,000 Klansmen within five days' notice, but as a secret or "invisible" group with no membership rosters, it was difficult to judge the Klan's actual size. The KKK has at times been politically powerful and at various times controlled the governments of Tennessee, Indiana, Oklahoma and Oregon, in addition to several legislatures in the South.

Europe

In 1867 the **Irish Republican Brotherhood**, a revolutionary Irish nationalist group, carried out attacks in England. Writer Richard English has referred to such attacks as the first acts of "republican terrorism," which would became a recurrent feature of British and Irish history. The group is considered a precursor to the Irish Republican Army.

Europeans invented **"Propaganda of the deed"** (or "propaganda by the deed," from the French *propagande par le fait*) theory, a concept that advocates physical violence or other provocative public acts against political enemies in order to inspire mass rebellion or revolution. An early proponent was the Italian revolutionary Carlo Pisacane (1818–1857), who wrote in his "Political Testament" (1857) that "ideas spring from deeds and not the other way around." Anarchist Mikhail Bakunin (1814–1876), in his "Letters to a Frenchman on the Present Crisis" (1870) stated that "we must spread our principles, not with words but with deeds, for this is the most popular, the most potent and the most irresistible form of propaganda." The phrase itself was popularized by the French anarchist Paul Brousse (1844–1912), who in 1877 cited as examples the 1871 Paris Commune and a workers' demonstration in Berne provocatively using the socialist red flag. By the 1880s, the slogan had begun to be used to refer to bombings, regicides and tyrannicides. Reflecting this new understanding of the term, Italian anarchist Errico Malatesta in 1895 described "propaganda by the deed" (which he opposed the use of) as violent communal insurrections meant to ignite an imminent revolution.

Founded in Russia in 1878, **Narodnaya Volya** was a revolutionary anarchist group inspired by Sergei Nechayev and "propaganda by the deed" theorist Pisacane. The group developed ideas—such as targeted killing of the 'leaders of oppression'—that were to become the hallmark of subsequent violence by small non-state groups and they were convinced that the developing technologies of the age—such as the invention of dynamite, which they were the first anarchist group to make widespread use of—enabled them to strike directly and with discrimination. Attempting to spark a popular revolt against Russia's Tsars, the group killed prominent political figures by gun and bomb and on March 13, 1881, assassinated Russia's Tsar Alexander II. The assassination, by a bomb that also killed the Tsar's attacker, Ignacy Hryniewiecki, failed to spark the expected revolution and an ensuing crackdown brought the group to an end.

Individual Europeans also engaged in politically motivated violence. For example, in 1893, Auguste Vaillant, a French anarchist, threw a bomb in the French Chamber of Deputies in which one person was injured. In reaction to Vaillant's bombing and other bombings and assassination attempts, the French government passed a set of laws restricting freedom of the press that were pejoratively known as the *lois scélérates* ("villainous laws"). From 1894 to 1896, President of France Marie Francois Carnot, Prime Minister of Spain Antonio Cánovas del Castillo and Austria-Hungary Empress Elisabeth of Bavaria were killed by anarchists.

The Ottoman Empire

Several nationalist groups used violence against an Ottoman Empire in apparent decline. One was the **Armenian Revolutionary Federation** (in Armenian *Dashnaktsuthium*, or "The Federation"), a revolutionary movement founded in Tiflis (Russian Transcaucasia) in 1890 by Christopher Mikaelian. Many members had been part of Narodnaya Volya or the Hunchakian Revolutionary Party. The group published newsletters, smuggled arms and hijacked buildings as it sought to bring in European intervention that would force the Ottoman Empire to surrender control of its Armenian territories. On August 24, 1896, 17-year-old Babken Suni led twenty-six members in capturing the Imperial Ottoman Bank in Constantinople. The group unsuccessfully demanded the creation of an Armenian state, but backed down on a threat to blow up the bank. An ensuing security crackdown destroyed the group.

Also inspired by Narodnaya Volya, the **Internal Macedonian Revolutionary Organization** (IMRO) was a revolutionary movement founded in 1893 by Hristo Tatarchev in the Ottoman-controlled Macedonian territories. Through assassinations and by provoking uprisings, the group sought to coerce the Ottoman government into creating a Macedonian nation. On July 20, 1903, the group incited the Ilinden uprising in the Ottoman villayet of Monastir. The IMRO declared the town's independence and sent demands to the European Powers that all of Macedonia be freed. The demands were ignored and Turkish troops crushed the 27,000 rebels in the town two months later.

Early 20th Century

Revolutionary nationalism continued to motivate political violence in the 20th century, much of it directed against the British Empire. The Irish Republican Army campaigned against the British in the 1910s and inspired the Zionist groups Hagannah, Irgun and Lehi to fight the British throughout the 1930s in the Palestine mandate. Like the IRA and the Zionist groups, the Muslim Brotherhood used bombings and assassinations to try to free Egypt from British control.

Europe

Political assassinations continued into the 20th century, its first victim Umberto I of Italy, killed in July 1900. Political violence became especially widespread in Imperial Russia and several ministers were killed in the opening years of the century. The highest ranking was Prime Minister Pyotr Stolypin, killed in 1911 by a leftist radical.

On June 28, 1914, Archduke Franz Ferdinand of Austria, heir to the Austro-Hungarian throne and his wife, Sophie, Duchess of Hohenberg, were shot and killed in Sarajevo, capital of Bosnia and Herzegovina, by Gavrilo Princip, one of a group of six assassins. The assassinations produced widespread shock across Europe, setting in motion a series of events which led to World War I.

In an action called the Easter Rising or Easter Rebellion, on April 24, 1916, members of the Irish Volunteers and Irish Citizen Army seized the Dublin General Post Office and several other buildings, proclaiming an independent Irish Republic. The rebellion failed militarily but was a success for physical force Irish republicanism, leaders of the uprising becoming Irish heroes after their eventual execution by the British government. Shortly after the rebellion, Michael Collins and others founded the **Irish Republican Army** (IRA), which from 1916 to 1923 carried out numerous attacks against symbols of British power. For example, it attacked over 300 police stations simultaneously just before Easter 1920, and, in November 1920, publicly killed a dozen police officers and burned down the Liverpool docks and warehouses, an action that came to be known as Bloody Sunday. After years of warfare, London agreed to the 1921 Anglo-Irish treaty creating an independent Irish nation encompassing 26 of the island's 32 counties. IRA tactics were an inspiration to other groups, including the Palestine Mandate's Zionists and to British special operations during World War II.

Middle East

Operating in the Palestine, **Irgun** was a clandestine militant Zionist group that split off from another militant group, **Hagannah**, in 1931. The group was founded by Avraham Tehomi, who was inspired by Ze'ev Jabotinsky's belief that only Jewish armed force would ensure the establishment of a Jewish state. Like Hagannah, Irgun sought to end British rule by assassinating police, capturing British government buildings and arms and sabotaging British railways. It also smuggled Jews into Palestine. Its tactic of attacking Arab communities, including bombing a crowded Arab market, is considered among the first examples of terrorism directed against civilians. Irgun's most famous attack was the 1946 bombing of the King David Hotel, the British Military headquarters in Jerusalem. Ninety-one people, both soldiers and civilians, were killed. After the creation of Israel in 1948, Menachem Begin (Irgun leader from 1943 to 1948) transformed the group into the political party which later became part of Likud.

Lehi (*Lohameni Herut Yisrael*, a.k.a. "Freedom Fighters for Israel," a.k.a. Stern Gang) was a revisionist Zionist group that splintered off from Irgun in 1940. Abraham Stern formed Lehi from disaffected Irgun members after Irgun agreed to a truce with Britain in 1940. Lehi assassinated prominent politicians as a strategy. For example, on November 6, 1944, Lord Moyne, the British Minister of State for the Middle East, was assassinated. The act was controversial among the Zionist militant groups, Hagannah sympathizing with the British and launching a massive man-hunt against the other Lehi and Irgun. After Israel's 1948 founding, Lehi was formally dissolved and its members integrated into the Israeli Defense Forces.

Germany and the Soviet Union of the 1930s

The 1930s saw the rise of totalitarian regimes in Stalin's Soviet Union and Hitler's Germany. Both regimes employed terror on an enormous scale. However and unlike some of the Jacobins who ruled France during its Reign of Terror, the regimes never applied the words 'terror' or 'terrorist' to the ruthless actions of their police, nor to the NKVD in the Soviet Union or the Gestapo in Nazi Germany, but only to those who opposed the two dictatorships. Historian R.J. Overy writes, "What is now defined as ruthless state terror was viewed by Hitler and Stalin as state protection against the enemies of the people." Effectively establishing and reinforcing obedience to regime and national ideology, both regimes used surveillance, imprisonment (often in Soviet gulags or German labour or concentration camps), torture and executions against enemies of the state real and imagined.

World War II

The Resistance Movement in Europe

Some of the tactics of the guerilla, partisan and resistance movements organised and supplied by the Allies during World War II, according to historian M.R.D. Foot, can be considered terrorist. Colin Gubbins, a key leader within the British Special Operations Executive (SOE), made sure the organisation drew much of its inspiration from the IRA. On the eve of D-Day, the SOE organised with the French resistance the complete destruction of the rail and communication infrastructure of western France perhaps the largest coordinated attack of its kind in history. Allied supreme commander Dwight Eisenhower later wrote that "the disruption of enemy rail communications, the harassing of

German road moves and the continual and increasing strain placed on German security services throughout occupied Europe by the organised forces of Resistance, played a very considerable part in our complete and final victory."

Aerial Bombardment and Civilians

Some scholars consider the deliberate bombardment of civilian populations a form of state terror, and, during the military conflicts leading up to World War II and the war itself, bombing of enemy civilian populations in order to terrorize and break morale was first employed. For example, aerial bombardment (the bombs often packed with mustard gas) was a major aspect of Italy's 1935 war against Ethiopia, as Italian forces were ordered by Benito Mussolini to "systematically conduct a politics of terror and extermination of the rebels and the complicit population."

Beginning early in the 1930s and with greatest intensity between 1938 and 1943, the Japanese used incendiary bombs against Chinese cities such as Shanghai, Wuhan and Chonging. Lord Cranborne, the British Under-Secretary of State For Foreign Affairs, commented on a 1937 bombing: "The military objective, where it exists, seems to take a completely second place. The main object seems to be to inspire terror by the indiscriminate slaughter of civilians..." In Europe in 1937, the bombardment of Guernica (April 26, 1937), carried out by Nazi Germany's Luftwaffe, caused widespread destruction and civilian deaths in the Basque town. According to the BBC, the goal of General Francisco Franco, commander of the nationalist forces during the Spanish Civil War, was "to terrorize the people in the Basque region. . ."

In May 1940, during World War II itself, the Luftwaffe forced Netherlands' surrender by bombing Rotterdam and threatening to do the same to Utrecht. In a bombing campaign against Britain called "the Blitz" (September 1940, to May

1941), Germany carried out intensive bombardment of British cities such as London and war industry centers such as Coventry. Britain, perhaps in response, adopted a bombing policy against German cities euphemistically called area bombardment, one of whose objectives was to 'de-house' and demoralize German civilians. The Dresden bombing (February 13–15, 1945) was an instance of area bombardment that left the city in ruins and claimed up to 40,000 lives. In its air attacks on Japan, U.S. forces used a mix of incendiaries and high explosives to burn to the ground large sections of Japanese cities. A military aide to General Douglas MacArthur called one incendiary attack on Tokyo "one of the most ruthless and barbaric killings of non-combatants in all history."

Mid-20th Century

After World War II, largely successful anti-colonial campaigns were launched against the collapsing European empires, as many World War II resistance groups became militantly anti-colonial. The Viet Minh, for example, which had fought against the Japanese, now fought the returning French colonists. In the Middle East, the Muslim Brotherhood used bombings and assassinations against British rule in Egypt. Also during the 1950s, the National Liberation Front (FLN) in French-controlled Algeria and the EOKA in British-controlled Cyprus waged guerilla and open war against colonial powers.

In the 1960s, inspired by Mao's Chinese revolution of 1949 and Castro's Cuban revolution of 1959, national independence movements in formerly colonized countries often fused nationalist and socialist impulses in the 1960s. This was the case with Spain's ETA, the Front de libération du Québec and the Palestine Liberation Organization.

In the late 1960s and 1970s violent leftist groups were on the rise, sympathizing with Third World guerrilla movements and seeking to spark anti-capitalist revolt. Such groups included the PKK in Turkey, Armenia's ASALA, the Japanese Red Army, the German Red Army Faction, the Italian Red Brigade, and, in the U.S., the Weather Underground. Nationalist groups such as the Provisional IRA and the Tamil tigers also began operations at this time.

Throughout the Cold War, both the U.S. and the Soviet Union made extensive use of violent nationalist organizations to carry on a war by proxy. For example, Soviet and Chinese military advisers provided training and support to the Viet Cong during the Vietnam War, while the U.S. funded groups such as the Contras in Nicaragua. Ironically, many violent Islamic militants of the late 20th and early 21st century had been funded in the 1980s by the US and the UK because they were fighting the USSR in Afghanistan.

Middle East

Founded in 1928 as a nationalist social-welfare and political movement in British-controlled Egypt, the **Muslim Brotherhood** in the late 1940s began to attack British soldiers and police stations. Founded and led by Hassan al-Banna, it also assassinated politicians seen as collaborating with British rule, most prominently Egyptian Prime Minister Nuqrashi in 1948. British rule was overthrown in a 1952 military coup and shortly thereafter the Muslim Brotherhood went underground in the face of a massive crackdown. Though sometimes banned or otherwise oppressed, the group continues to exist in present-day Egypt.

The ***Front de Liberation National*** (FLN) was a nationalist group founded in French-controlled Algeria in 1954. The group was a large-scale resistance movement against French occupation, with alleged terrorism only part of its operations. The FLN leadership was inspired by the Viet Minh rebels who had made French troops withdraw from Vietnam. The FLN was one of the first anti-colonial groups to use large scale compliance violence. The FLN would establish control over a rural village and coerce its peasants to execute any French loyalists among them. On the night of October 31, 1954, in a coordinated wave of seventy bombings and shootings known as the Toussaint attacks, the FLN attacked French military installations and the homes of Algerian loyalists. In the following year, the group gained significant support for an uprising against loyalists in Philipville. This uprising — and the heavy-handed response by the French — convinced many Algerians to support the FLN and the independence movement. The FLN eventually secured Algerian independence from France in 1962 and transformed itself into Algeria's ruling party.

Fatah was organized as a Palestinian nationalist group in 1954 and exists today as a political party in Palestine. In 1967 it joined the **Palestine Liberation Organization** (PLO), an umbrella organisation for secular Palestinian nationalist groups formed in 1964. The PLO began its own armed operations in 1965. The PLO's membership is made up of separate and possibly contending paramilitary and political factions, the largest of which are Fatah, PFLP and DFLP. Factions of the PLO have advocated or carried out acts of terrorism. Abu Iyad organised the Fatah splinter group Black September in 1970; the group is best known for seizing eleven Israeli athletes as hostages at the September 1972 Summer Olympics in Munich. All the athletes and five Black September operatives died during a gun battle with the West German police, in what was later known as the Munich massacre. The Popular Front for the Liberation of Palestine (PFLP) was founded in 1967 by George Habash and on September 6, 1970, the group hijacked three international passenger planes, landing two of them in Jordan and blowing up the third. Fatah leader and PLO Chairman Yasser Arafat publicly renounced terrorism in December 1988 on behalf of the PLO, but Israel has stated it has proof that Arafat continued to sponsor terrorism until his death in 2004.

The **People's Mujahidin of Iran** (PMOI) or Mujahedin-e-Khalq, is a socialist islamic group that has fought Iran's government since the Khomeini revolution. The group was originally founded to oppose capitalism and what it perceived as western exploitation of Iran under the Shah. The group would go on to play an important role in the Shah's overthrow but was unable to capitalize on this in the following power vacuum. The group is suspected of having a membership of between 10,000 and 30,000. The group renounced violence in 2001 but remains a proscribed terror organization in Iran and the U.S., The EU, however, has removed the group from its terror list. The PMOI is accused of supporting other groups such as the Jundallah.

The **Armenian Secret Army for the Liberation of Armenia** (ASALA) was founded in 1975 in Beirut during the Lebanese Civil War by Hagop Tarakchian and Hagop Hagopian with the help of sympathetic Palestinians. At the time, Turkey was in political turmoil and Hagopian believed that the time was right to avenge the Armenians who died during the Armenian Genocide and to force the Turkish government to cede the territory of Wilsonian Armenia to establish a nation state also incorporating the Armenian SSR. In its Esenboga airport attack, on 7 August 1982, two ASALA rebels opened fire on civilians in a waiting room at the Esenboga International Airport in Ankara. Nine people died and 82 were injured. By 1986, the ASALA had virtually ceased all attacks.

The "Partiya Karkerên Kurdistan" (**Kurdistan Workers Party** or PKK) was established in Turkey in 1978 as a Kurdish nationalist party. Founder Abdullah Ocalan Ocalan was inspired by the Maoist theory of people's war and like Algeria's FLN he advocated the use of compliance terror. The group seeks to create an independent Kurdish state consisting of parts of south-eastern Turkey, north-eastern Iraq, northeastern Syria and north-western Iran. In 1984, the PKK transformed itself into a paramilitary organisation and launched conventional attacks as well as bombings against Turkish governmental installations. In 1999, Turkish authorities captured Öcalan. He was tried in Turkey and sentenced to life imprisonment. The PKK has since gone through a series of name changes.

Europe

Founded in 1959 and still active, the **Euskadi Ta Askatasuna** is an armed Basque nationalist separatist organisation. Formed in response to General Francisco Franco's suppression of the Basque language and culture, ETA evolved from an advocacy group for traditional Basque culture into an armed Marxist group demanding Basque independence. Many ETA victims are government officials, the group's first known victim a police chief killed in 1968. In 1973 ETA operatives killed Franco's apparent successor, Admiral Luis Carrero Blanco, by planting an underground bomb under his habitual parking spot outside a Madrid church. In 1995, an ETA car bomb nearly killed Jose Maria Aznar, then the leader of the conservative Popular Party and the same year investigators disrupted a plot to assassinate King Juan Carlos. Efforts by Spanish governments to negotiate with the ETA have failed and in 2003 the Spanish Supreme Court banned the Batasuna political party, which was determined to be the political arm of ETA.

The **Provisional Irish Republican Army** was an Irish nationalist movement founded in December 1969 when several militants including Seán Mac Stíofáin broke-off from the Official IRA and formed a new organization. Led by Mac Stíofáin in the early 1970s and by a group around Gerry Adams since the late 1970s, the Provisional IRA sought to create an all-island Irish state. Between 1969 and 1997, during a period known as the Troubles, the group conducted an armed campaign, including bombings, gun attacks, assassinations and even a mortar attack on 10 Downing Street. On July 21, 1972, in an attack later known as Bloody Friday, the group set off twenty-two bombs, killing nine and injuring 130. On July 28, 2005, the Provisional IRA Army Council announced an end to its armed campaign. The IRA is believed to have been a major exporter of arms to and provided military training to groups such as the FARC in Colombia and the PLO . In the case of the latter there has been a long held solidarity movement, which is evident by the many murals around Belfast.

The **Red Army Faction** (RAF) was a New Leftist group founded in 1968 by Andreas Baader and Ulrike Meinhof in West Germany. Inspired by Che Guevara, Maoist socialism and the Vietcong, the group sought to raise awareness of the Vietnamese and Palestinian independence movements through kidnappings, taking embassies hostage, bank robberies, assassinations, bombings and attacks on U.S. air bases. The group is best known for 1977's "German Autumn." The buildup leading to German Autumn began on April 7, when the RAF shot Federal Prosecutor Siegfried Buback. On July 30, it shot Jurgen Ponto, then head of the Dresdner Bank, in a failed kidnapping attempt; on September 5, the group kidnapped Hanns Martin Schleyer (a former SS officer and an important West German industrialist), executing him on October 19. The hijacking of the Lufthansa jetliner "Lufthansa Flight 181" by the PFLP, a Palestinian group, is also considered to be part of German Autumn.

The **Italian Red Brigade** was a New Leftist group founded by Renato Curcio in 1970. With PLO support, the group sought to create a revolutionary state. The Brigade kidnapped former Prime Minister Aldo Moro on March 16, 1978 and killed him 56 days later. This inspired an all-out assault against the Brigade by Italian law enforcement and security forces and drew condemnation from Italian left-wing radicals and even from imprisoned ex-leaders of the Brigade. The Brigade lost most of its social support and public opinion turned strongly against it. In 1984, the Brigade split, the majority faction becoming the Communist Combatant Party (Red Brigades-PCC) and the minority faction reconstituting itself as the Union of Combatant Communists (Red Brigades-UCC). The members of these groups carried out a handful of assassinations before almost all were arrested in 1989.

The Americas

The **Front de libération du Québec** (FLQ) was a Marxist nationalist group that sought to create an independent, socialist Quebec. Georges Schoeters founded the group in 1963 and was inspired by Che Guevara and Algeria's FLN. The group was accused of bombings, kidnappings and assassinations of politicians, soldiers and civilians. On October 5, 1970, the FLQ kidnapped James Richard Cross, the British Trade Commissioner and on October 10, the Minister of Labour and Vice-Premier of Quebec, Pierre Laporte. Laporte was killed a week later. After these events support for violence in order to attain Quebec independence declined and support increased for the Parti Québécois, which took power in Quebec in 1976.

In Colombia several paramilitary groups formed during the 1960s and afterwards. In 1983, President Fernando Belaúnde Terry of Peru described armed attacks on his nation's anti-narcotics police as **"narcoterrorism"**, i.e., which refers to "violence waged by drug producers to extract political concessions from the government." Pablo Escobar's ruthless violence in his dealings with the Colombian and Peruvian governments has been probably one of the best known and best documented examples of narcoterrorism. Paramilitary groups associated with narcoterrorism include the Ejército de Liberación Nacional (ELN), the Fuerzas Armadas Revolucionarias de Colombia (FARC) and the Autodefensas

Unidas de Colombia (AUC). While the ELN and FARC were originally leftist revolutionary groups and the AUC was originally a right-wing paramilitary, all have conducted numerous attacks on civilians and civilian infrastructure and the U.S. and some European governments consider them terrorist organizations.

The **Jewish Defense League'** (JDL) was founded in 1969 by Rabbi Meir Kahane in New York City, with its declared purpose the protection of Jews from harassment and antisemitism. Federal Bureau of Investigation statistics state that, from 1980 to 1985, 15 attacks the FBI classified as acts of terrorism were attempted in the U.S. by members of the JDL. The National Consortium for the Study of Terror and Responses to Terrorism states that, during the JDL's first two decades of activity, it was an "active terrorist organization.". Kahane later founded the far-right Israeli political party Kach, which was banned from elections in Israel on the ground of racism. The JDL's present-day website condemns all forms of terrorism.

The ***Fuerzas Armadas de Liberación Nacional*** (FALN, "Armed Forces of National Liberation") is a nationalist group founded in Puerto Rico in 1974. Over the decade that followed the group used bombings and targeted killings of civilians and police in pursuit of an independent Puerto Rico. The FALN in 1975 took responsibility for four nearly simultaneous bombings in New York City. The United States Federal Bureau of Investigation (FBI) has classified the FALN as a terrorist organisation.

The Weather Underground (a.k.a. **the Weathermen**) began as a militant faction of the leftist Students for a Democratic Society (SDS) organization and in 1969 took over the organization. Weathermen leaders, inspired by China's Maoists, the Black Panthers and the 1968 student revolts in France, sought to raise awareness of its revolutionary anti-capitalist and anti-Vietnam War platform by destroying symbols of government power. From 1969 to 1974 the Weathermen bombed corporate offices, police stations and Washington government sites such as the Pentagon. After the end of the Vietnam War in 1975, most of the group disbanded.

Asia

The **Japanese Red Army** was founded by Fusako Shigenobu in Japan in 1971 and attempted to overthrow the Japanese government and start a world revolution. Allied with the Palestinian group PFLP, the group committed assassinations, hijacked a commercial Japanese aircraft and sabotaged a Shell oil refinery in Singapore. On May 30, 1972, Kôzô Okamoto and other group members launched a machine gun and grenade attack at Israel's Lod Airport in Tel Aviv, killing 26 people and injuring 80 others. Two of the three attackers then killed themselves with grenades.

Founded in 1976, the **Liberation Tigers of Tamil Eelam**, (also called "LTTE" or **Tamil Tigers**) was a militant Tamil nationalist political and paramilitary organisation based in northern Sri Lanka. From its founding by Velupillai Prabhakaran, it waged a secessionist resistance campaign that sought to create an independent Tamil state in the northern and eastern regions of Sri Lanka. The conflict originated in measures the majority Sinhalese took that were perceived as attempts to marginalize the Tamil minority.. The resistance campaign evolved into the Sri Lankan Civil War, one of the longest-running armed conflicts in Asia. The group carried out many bombings, including an April 21, 1987, car bomb attack at a Colombo bus terminal that killed 110 people. In 2009 the Sri Lankan military launched a major military offensive against the secessionist movement and claimed that it had effectively destroyed the LTTE.

Africa

Founded in 1961, **Umkhonto we Sizwe** (MK) was the military wing of the African National Congress; it waged a guerilla campaign against the South African apartheid regime and was responsible for many bombings. MK launched its first guerrilla attacks against government installations on 16 December 1961. South Africa subsequently banned the group after classifying it as a terrorist organization. MK's first leader was Nelson Mandela, who was tried and imprisoned for the group's acts. With the end of apartheid in South Africa, Umkhonto we Sizwe was incorporated into the South African armed forces.

Late 20th Century

In the 1980s and 1990s, Islamic militancy in pursuit of religious and political goals increased, many militants drawing inspiration from Iran's 1979 Islamic Revolution. In the 1990s, well-known violent acts that targeted civilians were the Tokyo subway sarin gas attack by Aum Shinrikyo and the bombing of Oklahoma City's Murrah Federal Building.

The Americas

The Contras were a counter-revolutionary militia formed in 1979 to oppose Nicaragua's Sandinista government. The Catholic Institute for International Relations asserted the following about contra operating procedures in 1987: "The record of the contras in the field . . . is one of consistent and bloody abuse of human rights, of murder, torture, mutilation, rape, arson, destruction and kidnapping." Americas Watch — subsequently folded into Human Rights Watch — accused the Contras of targeting health care clinics and health care workers for assassination; kidnapping civilians, torturing civilians; executing civilians, including children, who were captured in combat; raping women; indiscriminately attacking civilians and civilian houses; seizing civilian property and burning civilian houses in captured towns. The contras disbanded after the election of Violetta Chamorro in 1990.

The April 19, 1995, **Oklahoma City bombing** was directed at the U.S. government, according to the prosecutor at the murder trial of Timothy McVeigh, who was convicted of carrying out the crime. The bombing of the Alfred P. Murrah Federal Building in downtown Oklahoma City claimed 168 lives and left over 800 injured. McVeigh, who was convicted of first degree murder and executed, said his motivation was revenge for U.S. government actions at Waco and Ruby Ridge.

Middle East

Hezbollah ("Party of God") is an Islamic movement and political party founded in Lebanon shortly after that country's 1982 civil war. Inspired by Ayatollah Ruhollah Khomeini and the Iranian revolution, the group originally sought an Islamic revolution in Lebanon and has long fought for the withdrawal of Israeli forces from Lebanon. Led by Sheikh Sayyed Hassan Nasrallah since 1992, the group has kidnapped Israeli soldiers and carried out missile attacks and suicide bombings against Israeli military and civilian targets.

Egyptian Islamic Jihad (a.k.a. Al-Gamaa Al-Islamiyya) is a militant Egyptian Islamist movement dedicated to the establishment of an Islamic state in Egypt. The group formed in 1980 as an umbrella organisation for militant student groups formed after the leadership of the Muslim Brotherhood renounced violence. It is led by Omar Abdel-Rahman, who has been accused of participation in the World Trade Center 1993 bombings. In 1981, the group assassinated Egyptian President Anwar Sadat. On November 17, 1997, in what became known as the Luxor massacre, it attacked tourists at the Temple of Hatshepsut (Deir el-Bahri); six men dressed as police machine-gunned 58 Japanese and European vacationers and four Egyptians.

On December 21, 1988, **Pan Am Flight 103**, a Pan American World Airways flight from London's Heathrow International Airport to New York's John F. Kennedy International Airport, was destroyed mid flight over the Scottish town of Lockerbie. On January 31, 2001, Libyan Abdel Basset Ali al-Megrahi was convicted by a panel of three Scottish judges of bombing the flight and was sentenced to 27 years imprisonment. In 2002 Libya offered financial compensation to victims' families in exchange for lifting of UN and U.S. sanctions. In 2007 al-Megrahi was granted leave to appeal against his conviction and in August 2009 was released on compassionate grounds by the Scottish Executive due to his terminal cancer.

Hamas is an Islamic Palestinian group. Sheikh Ahmed Yassin, Abdel Aziz al-Rantissi and Mohammad Taha of the Palestinian wing of Egypt's Muslim Brotherhood created Hamas in 1987, at the beginning of the First Intifada, an uprising against Israeli rule in the Palestinian Territories. Beginning in 1993, Hamas launched numerous suicide bombings against Israel. On March 27, 2002, it bombed the Netanya hotel, killing 30. Hamas ceased suicide attacks in 2005 and renounced them in April 2006. Hamas has also been responsible for Israel-targeted rocket attacks, IED attacks and shootings, but it reduced most of those operations in 2005 and 2006. After winning legislative elections in the Palestinian Territories, Hamas has since June 2007 governed the Gaza portion of the territories.

February 25, 1994, Baruch Goldstein, an American-born Israeli physician, perpetrated the Cave of the Patriarchs massacre in the city of Hebron, Goldstein shot and killed between 30 and 54 Muslim worshippers inside the Ibrahimi Mosque (within the Cave of the Patriarchs) and wounded another 125 to 150. Goldstein, who was lynched and killed in the mosque, was a supporter of **Kach**, an Israeli political party founded by Rabbi Meir Kahane that advocated the expulsion of Arabs from Israel and the Palestinian Territories. In the aftermath of the Goldstein attack and Kach statements praising it, Kach was outlawed in Israel. Today, Kach and a breakaway group, Kahane Chai, are considered terrorist organisations by Israel, Canada, the European Union and the United States.

Asia

Aum Shinrikyo, now known as Aleph, was a Japanese religious group founded by Shoko Asahara in 1984 as a yogic meditation group. Later, in 1990, Asahara and 24 other members campaigned for election to the House of Representatives under the banner of Shinri-tô (Supreme Truth Party). None were voted in and the group began to militarize. Between 1990 and 1995, the group attempted several apparently unsuccessful violent attacks using the methods of biological warfare, using botulin toxin and anthrax spores. On June 28, 1994, Aum Shinrikyo members released sarin gas from several sites in the Kaichi Heights neighbourhood of Matsumoto, Japan, killing eight and injuring 200 in what became known as the Matsumoto incident. Seven months later, on March 20, 1995, Aum Shinrikyo members released sarin gas in a coordinated attack on five trains in the Tokyo subway system, killing 12 commuters and damaging the health of about 5,000 others in what became known as the subway sarin incident. In May 1995, Asahara and other senior leaders were arrested and the group's membership rapidly decreased.

Europe

Chechnyan separatists, led by Shamil Basayev, carried out several attacks on Russian targets between 1994 and 2006. In the June 1995 Budyonnovsk hospital hostage crisis, Basayev-led separatists took over 1,000 civilians hostage in a hospital in the southern Russian city of Budyonnovsk. When Russian special forces attempted to free the hostages, 105 civilians and 25 Russian troops were killed. In the 2002 Moscow theater hostage crisis, 50 Chechnyan separatists took 850 hostages in a Moscow theater, demanding the withdrawal of Russian forces from Chechnya and an end to the Second Chechen War.

On September 1, 2004, in what became known as the Beslan school hostage crisis, 32 Chechnyan separatists took 1,300 children and adults hostage at Beslan's School Number One. When Russian authorities did not comply with the rebel demands that Russian forces withdraw from Chechnya, 20 adult male hostages were shot. After two days of stalled negotiations, Russian special forces stormed the building. In the ensuing melee, over 300 hostages died, along with 19 Russian servicemen and all but perhaps one of the rebels. Basayev is believed to have participated in organizing the attack.

21st Century

Major events after the September 11, 2001 Attacks include the Moscow Theatre Siege, the 2003 Istanbul bombings, the Madrid train bombings, the Beslan school hostage crisis, the 2005 London bombings, the October 2005 New Delhi bombings and the 2008 Mumbai Hotel Siege.

Middle East

Osama bin Laden, closely advised by Egyptian Islamic Jihad leader Ayman al-Zawahiri, in 1988 founded **Al-Qaeda** (meaning "The Base"), an Islamic jihadist movement to replace Western-controlled or dominated Muslim countries with Islamic fundamentalist regimes. In pursuit of that goal, bin Laden issued a 1996 manifesto that vowed violent jihad against U.S. military forces based in Saudi Arabia.

On August 7, 1998, individuals associated with Al Qaeda and Egyptian Islamic Jihad carried out simultaneous bombings of two U.S. embassies in Africa which resulted in 224 deaths.

On October 12, 2000, Al-Qaeda carried out the USS Cole bombing, a suicide bombing of the U.S. Navy destroyer USS Cole harbored in the Yemeni port of Aden. The bombing killed seventeen U.S. sailors. The group's most well-known attack, however, took place on September 11, 2001.

On September 11, 2001, nineteen men affiliated with al-Qaeda hijacked four commercial passenger jet airliners, crashing two of them into the World Trade Center in New York City and one into the Pentagon. As a result of the attacks, the World Trade Center's twin towers completely collapsed and 2,973 victims and the 19 hijackers died.

The United States responded to the attacks by launching the War on Terror. Specifically, on October 7, 2001, it invaded Afghanistan to depose the Taliban, which had harboured al-Qaeda terrorists. On October 26, 2001, the U.S. enacted the Patriot Act, anti-terrorism legislation that expanded the powers of U.S. law enforcement and intelligence agencies. Many countries followed with similar legislation.

Formed in 2003, **Jundallah** is a Sunni insurgent group from the Baloch region of Iran and neighbouring Pakistan. It has committed numerous attacks within Iran, stating that it is fighting for the rights of the Sunni minority there. In 2005 the group attempted to assassinate Iran's Prime Minister, Mahmoud Ahmadinejad. The group takes credit for other bombings, including the 2007 Zahedan bombings. Iran and other sources accuse the group of being a front for or supported by other nations, in particular the U.S. and Pakistan.

●●

3
Terrorism and Behaviour

Terrorism is not new and even though it has been used since the beginning of recorded history it can be relatively hard to define. Terrorism has been described variously as both a tactic and strategy; a crime and a holy duty; a justified reaction to oppression and an inexcusable abomination. Obviously, a lot depends on whose point of view is being represented. Terrorism has often been an effective tactic for the weaker side in a conflict. As an asymmetric form of conflict, it confers coercive power with many of the advantages of military force at a fraction of the cost. Due to the secretive nature and small size of terrorist organizations, they often offer opponents no clear organization to defend against or to deter.

That is why preemption is being considered to be so important. In some cases, terrorism has been a means to carry on a conflict without the adversary realizing the nature of the threat, mistaking terrorism for criminal activity. Because of these characteristics, terrorism has become increasingly common among those pursuing extreme goals throughout the world. But despite its popularity, terrorism can be a nebulous concept. Even within the U.S. Government, agencies responsible for different functions in the ongoing fight against terrorism use different definitions.

The United States Department of Defense defines terrorism as "the calculated use of unlawful violence or threat of unlawful violence to inculcate fear; intended to coerce or to intimidate governments or societies in the pursuit of goals that are generally political, religious, or ideological." Within this definition, there are three key elements—violence, fear and intimidation—and each element produces terror in its victims. The FBI uses this: "Terrorism is the unlawful use of force and violence against persons or property to intimidate or coerce a government, the civilian population, or any segment thereof, in furtherance of political or social objectives." The U.S. Department of State defines "terrorism" to be "premeditated politically-motivated violence perpetrated against non-combatant targets by sub-national groups or clandestine agents, usually intended to influence an audience.

Outside the United States Government, there are greater variations in what features of terrorism are emphasized in definitions. The United Nations produced this definition in 1992; "An anxiety-inspiring method of repeated violent action, employed by (semi-) clandestine individual, group or state actors, for idiosyncratic, criminal or political reasons, whereby — in contrast to assassination — the direct targets of violence are not the main targets." The most commonly accepted academic definition starts with the U.N. definition quoted above and adds two sentences totaling another 77 words on the end; containing such verbose concepts as "message generators" and 'violence based communication processes." Less specific and considerably less verbose, the British Government definition of 1974 is"...the use of violence for political ends and includes any use of violence for the purpose of putting the public, or any section of the public, in fear."

Terrorism is a criminal act that influences an audience beyond the immediate victim. The strategy of terrorists is to commit acts of violence that draws the attention of the local populace, the government and the world to their cause. The terrorists plan their attack to obtain the greatest publicity, choosing targets that symbolize what they oppose. The effectiveness of the terrorist act lies not in the act itself, but in the public's or government's reaction to the act. For example, in 1972 at the Munich Olympics, the Black September Organisation killed 11 Israelis. The Israelis were the immediate victims. But the true target was the estimated 1 billion people watching the televised event.

The Black September Organization used the high visibility of the Olympics to publicize its views on the plight of the Palestinian refugees. Similarly, in October 1983, Middle Eastern terrorists bombed the Marine Battalion Landing Team Headquarters at Beirut International Airport. Their immediate victims were the 241 U.S. military personnel who were killed and over 100 others who were wounded. Their true target was the American people and the U.S. Congress. Their one act of violence influenced the United States' decision to withdraw the Marines from Beirut and was therefore considered a terrorist success.

There are three perspectives of terrorism: the terrorist's, the victim's and the general public's. The phrase "one man's terrorist is another man's freedom fighter" is a view terrorists themselves would accept. Terrorists do not see themselves as evil. They believe they are legitimate combatants, fighting for what they believe in, by whatever means possible. A victim of a terrorist act sees the terrorist as a criminal with no regard for human life. The general public's view is the most unstable. The terrorists take great pains to foster a "Robin Hood" image in hope of swaying the general public's point of view toward their cause. This sympathetic view of terrorism has become an integral part of their psychological warfare and needs to be countered vigorously.

Terrorist acts or the threat of such action have been in existence for millennia. Despite having a history longer than the modern nation-state, the use of terror by governments and those that contest their power remains poorly understood. While the meaning of the word terror itself is clear, when it is applied to acts and actors in the real world it becomes confused. Part of this is due to the use of terror tactics by actors at all levels in the social and political environment. Is the Unabomber, with his solo campaign of terror, a criminal, terrorist, or revolutionary?

Can he be compared to the French revolutionary governments who coined the word terrorism by instituting systematic state terror against the population of France in the 1790s, killing thousands? Are either the same as revolutionary terrorist groups such as the Baader-Mienhof Gang of West Germany or the Weather Underground in the United States?

So we see that distinctions of size and political legitimacy of the actors using terror raise questions as to what is and is not terrorism. The concept of moral equivalency is frequently used as an argument to broaden and blur the definition of terrorism as well. This concept argues that the outcome of an action is what matters, not the intent. Collateral or unintended damage to civilians from an attack by uniformed military forces on a legitimate military target is the same as a terrorist bomb directed deliberately at the civilian target with the intent of creating that damage.

Simply put, a car bomb on a city street and a jet fighter dropping a bomb on a tank are both acts of violence that produce death and terror. Therefore (at the extreme end of this argument) any military action is simply terrorism by a different name. This is the reasoning behind the famous phrase "One man's terrorist is another man's freedom fighter". It is also a legacy of legitimizing the use of terror by successful revolutionary movements after the fact.

The very flexibility and adaptability of terror throughout the years has contributed to the confusion. Those seeking to disrupt, reorder or destroy the status quo have continuously sought new and creative ways to achieve their goals. Changes in the tactics and techniques of terrorists have been significant, but even more significant are the growth in the number of causes and social contexts where terrorism is used.

Over the past 20 years, terrorists have committed extremely violent acts for alleged political or religious reasons. Political ideology ranges from the far left to the far right. For example, the far left can consist of groups such as Marxists and Leninists who propose a revolution of workers led by a revolutionary elite. On the far right, we find dictatorships that typically believe in a merging of state and business leadership.

Nationalism is the devotion to the interests or culture of a group of people or a nation. Typically, nationalists share a common ethnic background and wish to establish or regain a homeland.

Religious extremists often reject the authority of secular governments and view legal systems that are not based on their religious beliefs as illegitimate. They often view modernization efforts as corrupting influences on traditional culture.

Special interest groups include people on the radical fringe of many legitimate causes; e.g., people who use terrorism to uphold antiabortion views, animal rights, radical environmentalism. These groups believe that violence is morally justifiable to achieve their goals.

TERRORIST BEHAVIOUR

There is clearly a wide choice of definitions for terrorism. Despite this, there are elements in common among the majority of useful definitions. Common threads of the various definitions identify *terrorism* as:

- Political
- Psychological

- Coercive
- Dynamic
- Deliberate

Political

A terrorist act is a political act or is committed with the intention to cause a political effect. Clausewitz' statement that "war is a continuation of policy by other means" is taken as a truism by terrorists. They merely eliminate the intermediate step of armies and warfare and apply violence directly to the political contest.

Psychological

The intended results of terrorist acts cause a psychological effect ("terror"). They are aimed at a target audience other than the actual victims of the act. The intended target audience of the terrorist act may be the population as a whole, some specific portion of a society (an ethnic minority, for example), or decision-making elites in the society's political, social, or military populace.

Coercive

Violence and destruction are used in the commission of the act to produce the desired effect. Even if casualties or destruction are not the result of a terrorist operation, the threat or potential of violence is what produces the intended effect. For example, a successful hostage taking operation may result in all hostages being freed unharmed after negotiations and bargaining. Regardless of the outcome, the terrorist bargaining chips were nothing less than the raw threat of applying violence to maim or kill some or all of the hostages. When the threat of violence is not credible, or the terrorists are unable to implement violence effectively, terrorism fails.

Dynamic

Terrorist groups demand change, revolution, or political movement. The radical worldview that justifies terrorism mandates drastic action to destroy or alter the status quo. Even if the goals of a movement are reactionary in nature, they require action to "turn back the clock" or restore some cherished value system that is extinct. Nobody commits violent attacks on strangers or innocents to keep things "just the way they are."

Deliberate

Terrorism is an activity planned and intended to achieve particular goals. It is a rationally employed, specifically selected tactic and is not a random act. Since the victims of terrorist violence are often of little import, with one being as good for the terrorists' purposes as another, victim or target selection can appear random or unprovoked. But the target will contain symbolic value or be capable of eliciting emotional response according to the terrorists' goals. Remember that the actual target of terrorism is not the victim of the violence, but the psychological balance.

Media Exploitation

Terrorism's effects are not necessarily aimed at the victims of terrorist violence. Victims are usually objects to be exploited by the terrorists for their effect on a third party. In order to produce this effect, information of the attack must reach the target audience. So any terrorist organisation plans for exploitation of available media to get the message to the right audiences. Victims are simply the first medium that transmits the psychological impact to the larger target audience. The next step in transmission will depend on what media is available, but it will be planned and it will frequently be the responsibility of a specific organisation within the terrorist group to do nothing else but exploit and control the news cycle.

Some organizations can rely on friendly or sympathetic news outlets, but this is not necessary. News media can be manipulated by planning around the demands of the "news cycle" and the advantage that control of the initiative gives the terrorist. Pressures to report quickly, to "scoop" competitors, allow terrorists to present claims or make statements that might be refuted or critically commented on if time were available. Terrorists often provide names and details of individual victims to control the news media through its desire to humanize or personalize a story. For the victims of a terrorist attack, it is a certainty that the impact on the survivors (if there are any) is of minimal importance to the terrorists. What is important is the intended psychological impact that the news of their death or suffering will cause in a wider audience.

Operations in Permissive Societies

Terrorists conduct more operations in societies where individual rights and civil legal protections prevail. While terrorists may base themselves in repressive regimes that are sympathetic to them, they usually avoid repressive governments when conducting operations wherever possible. An exception to this case is a repressive regime that does not have the means to enforce security measures. Governments with effective security forces and few guaranteed civil liberties have typically suffered much less from terrorism than liberal states with excellent security forces. Al Qaeda has shown, however, that they will conduct operations anywhere.

Illegality of Methods

Terrorism is a criminal act. Whether the terrorist chooses to identify himself with military terminology (as discussed under insurgencies below), or with civilian imagery ("brotherhood", "committee", etc.), he is a criminal in both spheres. The violations of civil criminal laws are self-evident in activities such as murder, arson and kidnapping regardless of the legitimacy of the government enforcing the laws. Victimizing the innocent is criminal injustice under a dictatorship or a democracy. If the terrorist claims that he is justified in using such violence as a military combatant, he is a de facto war criminal under international law and the military justice systems of most nations.

Preparation and Support

It's important to understand that actual terrorist operations are the result of extensive preparation and support operations. Media reporting and academic study have mainly focused on the terrorists' goals and actions, which is precisely what the terrorist intends. This neglects the vital but less exciting topic of preparation and support operations. Significant effort and coordination is required to finance group operations, procure or manufacture weapons, conduct target surveillance and analysis and deliver trained terrorists to the operational area. While the time and effort expended by the terrorists may be a drop in the bucket compared to the amounts spent to defend against them, terrorist operations can still involve large amounts of money and groups of people. The need for dedicated support activities and resources on simple operations are significant and get larger the greater the sophistication of the plan and the complexity of the target.

Differences between Terrorism and Insurgency

If no single definition of terrorism produces a precise, unambiguous description, we can approach the question by eliminating similar activities that are not terrorism, but that appear to overlap. For the U.S. military, two such related concepts probably lead to more confusion than others. Guerilla warfare and insurgencies are often assumed to be synonymous with terrorism. One reason for this is that insurgencies and terrorism often have similar goals. However, if we examine insurgency and guerilla warfare, specific differences emerge.

A key difference is that an **insurgency is a movement** — a political effort with a specific aim. This sets it apart from both guerilla warfare and terrorism, as they are both methods available to pursue the goals of the political movement.

Another difference is the intent of the component activities and operations of insurgencies versus terrorism. There is nothing inherent in either insurgency or guerilla warfare that requires the use of terror. While some of the more successful insurgencies and guerilla campaigns employed terrorism and terror tactics and some developed into conflicts where terror tactics and terrorism became predominant; there have been others that effectively renounced the use of terrorism. The deliberate choice to use terrorism considers its effectiveness in inspiring further resistance, destroying government efficiency and mobilizing support. Although there are places where terrorism, guerilla warfare and criminal behaviour all overlap, groups that are exclusively terrorist, or subordinate "wings" of insurgencies formed to specifically employ terror tactics, demonstrate clear differences in their objectives and operations. Disagreement on the costs of using terror tactics, or whether terror operations are to be given primacy within the insurgency campaign, have frequently led to the "urban guerilla" or terrorist wings of an insurgency splintering off to pursue the revolutionary goal by their own methods.

The ultimate goal of an insurgency is to challenge the existing government for control of all or a portion of its territory, or force political concessions in sharing political power. Insurgencies require the active or tacit support of some portion of the population involved. External support, recognition or approval from other countries or political entities can be useful to insurgents, but is not required. A terror group does not require and rarely has the active support or even the sympathy of a large fraction of the population. While insurgents will frequently describe themselves as "insurgents" or "guerillas", terrorists will not refer to themselves as "terrorists" but describe themselves using military or political terminology ("freedom fighters", "soldiers", "activists"). Terrorism relies on public impact and is therefore conscious of the advantage of avoiding the negative connotations of the term "terrorists" in identifying themselves.

Terrorism does not attempt to challenge government forces directly, but acts to change perceptions as to the effectiveness or legitimacy of the government itself. This is done by ensuring the widest possible knowledge of the acts of terrorist violence among the target audience. Rarely will terrorists attempt to "control" terrain, as it ties them to identifiable locations and reduces their mobility and security. Terrorists as a rule avoid direct confrontations with government forces. A guerilla force may have something to gain from a clash with a government combat force, such as proving that they can effectively challenge the military effectiveness of the government. A terrorist group has nothing to gain from such a clash. This is not to say that they do not target military or security forces, but that they will not engage in anything resembling a "fair fight", or even a "fight" at all. Terrorists use methods that neutralize the strengths of conventional forces. Bombings and mortar attacks on civilian targets where military or security personnel spend off-duty time, ambushes of undefended convoys and assassinations of poorly protected individuals are common tactics.

Insurgency need not require the targeting of non-combatants, although many insurgencies expand the accepted legal definition of combatants to include police and security personnel in addition to the military. Terrorists do not discriminate between combatants and non-combatants, or if they do, they broaden the category of "combatants" so much as to render it meaningless. Defining all members of a nation or ethnic group, plus any citizen of any nation that supports that nation as "combatants" is simply a justification for frightfulness. Deliberate de-humanization and criminalization of the enemy in the terrorists' mind justifies extreme measures against anyone identified as hostile. Terrorists often expand their groups of acceptable targets and conduct operations against new targets without any warning or notice of hostilities.

Ultimately, the difference between insurgency and terrorism comes down to the intent of the actor. Insurgency movements and guerilla forces can adhere to international norms regarding the law of war in achieving their goals, but terrorists are by definition conducting crimes under both civil and military legal codes. Terrorists routinely claim that were they to adhere to any "law of war" or accept any constraints on the scope of their violence, it would place them at a disadvantage vis-à-vis the establishment. Since the nature of the terrorist mindset is absolutist, their goals are of paramount importance and any limitations on a terrorist's means to prosecute the struggle are unacceptable.

State Sponsored Terrorism

Is there a difference between terrorism and the use of specific tactics that exploit fear and terror by authorities normally considered "legitimate"? Nations and states often resort to violence to influence segments of their population, or rely on coercive aspects of state institutions. Just like the idea of equating any act of military force with terrorism described above, there are those who equate any use of government power or authority versus any part of the population as terrorism. This view also blurs the lines of what is and is not terrorism, as it elevates outcomes over intentions. Suppression of a riot by law enforcement personnel may in fact expose some of the population (the rioters) to violence and fear, but with the intent to protect the larger civil order. On the other hand, abuse of the prerogative of legitimized violence by the authorities is a crime.

But there are times when national governments will become involved in terrorism, or utilize terror to accomplish the objectives of governments or individual rulers. Most often, terrorism is equated with "non-state actors", or groups that are not responsible to a sovereign government. However, internal security forces can use terror to aid in repressing dissent and intelligence or military organizations perform acts of terror designed to further a state's policy or diplomatic efforts abroad.

A government that is an adversary of the United States may apply terror tactics and terrorism in an effort to add depth to their engagement of U.S. forces. Repression through terror of the indigenous population would take place to prevent internal dissent and insurrection that the U.S. might exploit. Military special operations assets and state intelligence operatives could conduct terrorist operations against U.S. interests both in theater and as far abroad as their capabilities allow. Finally, attacks against the U.S. homeland could be executed by state sponsored terrorist organizations or by paid domestic proxies. Three different ways that states can engage in the use of terror are:

- Governmental or "State" terror
- State involvement in terror
- State sponsorship of terrorism

Governmental or "State" terror: Sometimes referred to as "terror from above", where a government terrorizes its own population to control or repress them. These actions usually constitute the acknowledged policy of the government and make use of official institutions such as the judiciary, police, military and other government agencies. Changes to legal codes permit or encourage torture, killing, or property destruction in pursuit of government policy. After assuming power, official Nazi policy was aimed at the deliberate destruction of "state enemies" and the resulting intimidation of the rest of the population. Stalin's "purges" of the 1930s are examples of using the machinery of the state to terrorize a population. The methods he used included such actions as rigged show trials of opponents, punishing family or friends of suspected enemies of the regime and extra-legal use of police or military force against the population.

Saddam Hussein used chemical weapons on his own Kurdish population without any particular change or expansion of policies regarding the use of force on his own citizens. They were simply used in an act of governmental terror believed to be expedient in accomplishing his goals.

State involvement in terror: These are activities where government personnel carry out operations using terror tactics. These activities may be directed against other nations' interests, its own population, or private groups or individuals viewed as dangerous to the state. In many cases, these activities are terrorism under official sanction, although such authorization is rarely acknowledged openly. Historical examples include the Soviet and Iranian assassination campaigns against dissidents who had fled abroad and Libyan and North Korean intelligence operatives downing airliners on international flights.

Another type of these activities is "death squads" or "war veterans": unofficial actions taken by officials or functionaries of a regime (such as members of police or intelligence organizations) against their own population to repress or intimidate. While these officials will not claim such activities and disguise their participation, it is often made clear that they are acting for the state. Keeping such activities "unofficial" permits the authorities deniability and avoids the necessity of changing legal and judicial processes to justify oppression. This is different than "pro-state" terror, which is conducted by groups or persons with no official standing and without official encouragement. While pro-state terror may result in positive outcomes for the authorities, their employment of criminal methods and lack of official standing can result in disavowal and punishment of the terrorists, depending on the morality of the regime in question.

State sponsorship of terrorism: Also known as "state supported" terrorism, when governments provide supplies, training and other forms of support to non-state terrorist organizations. One of the most valuable types of this support is the provision of safe haven or physical basing for the terrorists' organisation. Another crucial service a state sponsor can provide is false documentation, not only for personal identification (passports, internal identification documents), but also for financial transactions and weapons purchases. Other means of support are access to training facilities and expertise not readily available to groups without extensive resources. Finally, the extension of diplomatic protections and services, such as immunity from extradition, diplomatic passports, use of embassies and other protected grounds and diplomatic pouches to transport weapons or explosives have been significant to some groups.

An example of state sponsorship is the Syrian government's support of Hamas and Hizballah in Lebanon. Syrian resources and protection enable the huge training establishments in the Bek'aa Valley. On a smaller, more discreet scale, the East German Stasi provided support and safe-haven to members of the Red Army Faction (RAF or Baader Meinhof Gang) and neo-fascist groups that operated in West Germany.

Wanted members of the RAF were found resident in East Germany after the fall of the Berlin Wall in 1989.

COUNTRIES WITH LARGE TERRORISM PRESENCE

Terrorists have long found refuge in countries and in many cases worked hand in hand with the local governments. Today several countries continue to attract terrorists for training and consipiring their attacks. The host countries do not try to disassociate themselves fully from their ties to terrorism and in some cases continue to provide tacit support and use terror to accomplish broader objectives. Some of the countries with significant terrorist operations include:

Afghanistan

Afghanistan became the hotbed of Islamic terror activities in the mid-1990s. With the radical Taliban government establishing control, several radical Islamic (mostly Sunni) terror organizations used Afghanistan as their training and operational base. Al Qaeda was the broad umbrella organisation that recruited terrorists from Pakistan, Afghanistan, Central Asia and around the world, training them in Afghanistan and Pakistan. Some of the terrosist groups still operating in the region include Al Qaeda, Al-Jihad, Lashkar-i-Jhangvi, Islamic Group, Armed Islamic Group, Harkat-ul-Mujahideen and the Islamic Movement of Uzbekistan.

Iran

Iran has long been an active sponsor of Islamic terrorism, including accusations of it supporting subversive activities in Iraq. Islamic Revolutionary Guard Corps and Ministry of Intelligence and Security were involved in the planning of and support for terrorist acts and continued to exhort a variety of groups that use terrorism to pursue their goals. Several terrorist groups including Lebanese Hizballah,

HAMAS, the Palestine Islamic Jihad and Ahmad Jibril's PFLP-GC have been provided funding, safehaven, training and weapons in Iran.

Iraq

Since the US led invasion of Iraq, the country has fallen into a violent spiral. The presence of US troops has attracted Islamic terrorists from the Middle-East and around the world. Al-Qaeda is believed to have established a toe-hold in the country along with various splinter groups. Some of the other terror organizations active in Iraq include Ansar al-Islam, Al-Faruq Brigades, Al-Mahdi Army, Iraqi Resistance Islamic Front (JAMI), Jamaat al-Tawhid wa'l-Jihad, Jaysh Muhammad and Kurdistan People's Congress (KHK).

Pakistan

Pakistan has long been a staging ground and planning centre for Islamic terrorists operating in South Asia. After the launch of Operation Enduring Freedom, thousands of terrorists were either killed or driven out of Afghansistan, mostly finding refuge in Pakistan. Pakistan and its secret service (ISI) have also been accused of training and funding several terrorist groups operating in Indian Kashmir. To many the links are clear, since the terrorist groups based in Pakistan operate in plain sight and have a distinct Indian focus. More recently, groups aligned with Al Qaeda and based in Pakistan have been responsbile for numerous terrorist attacks in Afghanistan. Some of these terror groups include Lashkar-e-Taiba, Jaish-e-Muhammad, Lashkar-e-Jhangvi, Al Qaeda, Tehreek-e-Jaferia, Sipah-e-Sahaba, Al Badr, Harkat ul-Ansar, Hizb-ul-Mujahideen, Tehreek-e-Nafaz-e-Shariat-e-Mohammadi, Jamaat ul-Fuqra and Muslim United Army.

Syria

Even as Syria continues to reduce its presence in Lebanon, it also continues to fund and host Palestinian and possibly

Iraqi terrorist organizations. HAMAS, the PIJ, the Popular Front for the Liberation of Palestine-General Command and the Popular Front for the Liberation of Palestine continue to operate from Syria.

Sudan

The African country of Sudan been a training hub and safe haven for members of several of the more violent international terrorist and radical Islamic groups of the last decade. Among the terror groups known to have operated from Sudan are Hezbollah (Party of God), Palestine Islamic Jihad, Abu Nidal Organization, HAMAS (Islamic Resistance Movement) and several smaller Islamic insurgent groups operating regionally in Ethiopia, Eritrea, Uganda and Tunisia.

GOALS AND MOTIVATIONS OF TERRORISTS

Ideology and motivation will influence the objectives of terrorist operations, especially regarding the casualty rate. Groups with secular ideologies and non-religious goals will often attempt highly selective and discriminate acts of violence to achieve a specific political aim. This often requires them to keep casualties at the minimum amount necessary to attain the objective. This is both to avoid a backlash that might severely damage the organisation and also maintain the appearance of a rational group that has legitimate grievances. By limiting their attacks they reduce the risk of undermining external political and economic support. Groups that comprise a "wing" of an insurgency, or are affiliated with aboveground, sometimes legitimate, political organizations often operate under these constraints. The tensions caused by balancing these considerations are often a prime factor in the development of splinter groups and internal factions within these organizations.

In contrast, religiously oriented and millenarian groups typically attempt to inflict as many casualties as possible.

Because of the apocalyptic frame of reference they use, loss of life is irrelevant and more casualties are better. Losses among their co-religionists are of little account, because such casualties will reap the benefits of the afterlife. Likewise, non-believers, whether they are the intended target or collateral damage, deserve death and killing them may be considered a moral duty. The Kenyan bombing against the U.S. Embassy in 1998 inflicted casualties on the local inhabitants in proportion to U.S. personnel of over twenty to one killed and an even greater disparity in the proportion of wounded (over 5000 Kenyans were wounded by the blast; 95% of total casualties were non-American). Fear of backlash rarely concerns these groups, as it is often one of their goals to provoke overreaction by their enemies and hopefully widen the conflict.

The type of target selected will often reflect motivations and ideologies. For groups professing secular political or social motivations, their targets are highly symbolic of authority; government offices, banks, national airlines and multinational corporations with direct relation to the established order. Likewise, they conduct attacks on representative individuals whom they associate with economic exploitation, social injustice, or political repression. While religious groups also use much of this symbolism, there is a trend to connect it to greater physical devastation. There also is a tendency to add religiously affiliated individuals, such as missionaries and religious activities, such as worship services, to the targeting equation.

Another common form of symbolism utilized in terrorist targeting is striking on particular anniversaries or commemorative dates. Nationalist groups may strike to commemorate battles won or lost during a conventional struggle, whereas religious groups may strike to mark particularly appropriate observances. Many groups will attempt to commemorate anniversaries of successful operations, or the executions or deaths of notable individuals related to their particular conflict. Likewise, striking on days of particular significance to the enemy can also provide the required impact. Since there are more events than operations, assessment of the likelihood of an attack on a commemorative date is only useful when analyzed against the operational pattern of a particular group or specific members of a group's leadership cadre.

The Intent of Terrorist Groups

A terrorist group commits acts of violence to –

- Produce widesrpead fear
- Obtain worldwide, national, or local recognition for their cause by attracting the attention of the media
- Harass, weaken, or embarrass government security forces so that the the government overreacts and appears repressive
- Steal or extort money and equipment, especially weapons and ammunition vital to the operation of their group
- Destroy facilities or disrupt lines of communication in order to create doubt that the government can provide for and protect its citizens
- Discourage foreign investments, tourism, or assistance programmes that can affect the target country's economy and support of the government in power
- Influence government decisions, legislation, or other critical decisions
- Free prisoners

- Satisfy vengeance
- Turn the tide in a guerrilla war by forcing government security forces to concentrate their efforts in urban areas. This allows the terrorist group to establish itself among the local populace in rural areas.

4
Terrorism: A Modern Scourge

Terrorism has become a part of modern life. Hijackings, bombings and assassinations on different continents of the world may seem like isolated attacks, but they reflect an easy reliance on violence as a way to promote social, political and religious change. They are elements of a pervasive end justifies the means philosophy being followed to its most perverse conclusions.

International terrorism has become the scourge of all democratic governments. These democratic governments are accustomed to dealing within a legal structure, often find it difficult to deal with criminals and terrorists that routinely operate outside of the law. However, deterrence is just as much a part of justice as proper enforcement of the laws. Democratic governments that do not deter criminals inevitably spawn vigilantism as normally law-abiding citizens who have lost confidence in the criminal justice system take the law into their own hands. A similar backlash is beginning to emerge as a result of the inability of western democracies to defend themselves against terrorists. However, lack of governmental resolve is only part of the problem.

Terrorists thrive on media exposure and news organizations around the world have been all too willing to give terrorists what they crave, publicity. If the news media gave terrorists the minuscule coverage their numbers and influence would decline. But, when hijackings and bombings are given prominent media attention, governments start feeling pressure from their citizens to resolve the crisis and eventually capitulate to terrorists' demands. News commentators have been unwilling to call terrorism what it is, Blind criminal violence. They soften their barbaric acts by arguing that one man's terrorist is another man's freedom fighter. This illusion is simply not true. Terrorists are not concerned about human rights and human dignity.

In fact, they end up destroying human rights in their alleged fight for human rights. A relatively new term for terrorism has been coined, new warfare. Yet, terrorists turn the notion of war on its head. Innocent citizens become targets in the devastating terrorist attacks. How do we define a terrorist? Is a terrorist a common criminal? If terrorists are mere criminals, then with reference to the Bible, they should be dealt with by their host governments. In Romans 13, the Apostle Paul says; He who resists authority has opposed the ordinance of God and they who have opposed will receive condemnation upon themselves. For rulers are not a cause of fear for good behaviour, but for evil. Do you want to have no fear of authority? Do what is good and you will have praise from the same; for it is a minister of God to you for good. But if you do what is evil, be afraid: for it does not bear the sword for nothing; for it is a minister of God, an avenger who brings wrath upon the one who practices evil This passage of scripture helps us make an important distinction we will use in our analysis of terrorism. It shows us that criminals are those who do evil and threaten the civil peace. But, any outside threat to the existence of the country is not a criminal threat but an act of war, which is also to be dealt with by the government.

In other words, criminals threaten the state from within. Foreign armies threaten the state from outside. These evildoers should live in fear of government. However, terrorists do not live in fear of the governing authorities in the countries where they live.

Meetings and negotiations haven't been able to strike fear in the hearts of terrorists. When we fight terrorism we need to realise we are talking about war. Military warfare is different from civilian peacekeeping. In civilian peacekeeping, people are presumed innocent until proven guilty. A citizen can be arrested and detained before trial but must be released unless guilt is proven. Military warfare is different. A trial is not held for each military action. In a sense, in a just war, a trial of sorts is held before any action is taken. Discussion and debates among government officials usually occur before war is declared. Fact-finding studies, presentations, testimonies and other kinds of forethought go into a declaration of war. In a sense, when the use of the military is involved, the trial period comes before anyone is confronted or arrested. But once war is declared, there are no more trials until the enemy is defeated. And every one who aids and abets the enemy is guilty by association. At present, terrorism is a one-sided war that the target governments are loosing. Soldiers and citizens are being killed in the war. Unfortunately, the target governments are not treating terrorism like the war it is. If we take the United States as an example, the limited war powers granted to the President by Congress are not powerful enough and are not used in a systematic way to defeat the enemy. If we are to win the war against terrorism, we must realise that it is war. Until we see it as military aggression, we will be unsuccessful in ending terrorism in this decade. If we continue on with the example of the United States, The ability of these groups to carry out their agenda is not the issue.

The fundamental issue is how U.S. government leaders should deal with this new type of military strategy. Terrorists have held American diplomats hostage for years, blown up military compounds and hijacked aeroplanes and cruise ships. Although some hostages have been released, many others have been killed and the U.S. has been unsuccessful at punishing more than a small number of terrorists. Even though international diplomacy has been the primary means used by The United States against terrorism, we should consider what other means may be appropriate. In the past, American leaders have responded to military aggression in a variety of ways short of declaring war. The U.S. Constitution grants the following powers to Congress: To define and punish piracies and felonies committed on the high Seas and offences against the law of nations; to declare war, grant letters of marquee and reprisal and make rules concerning captures on land and water. Terrorist acts fall into at least two of the congressional provisions for dealing with attacks on the nations. They are: (1) to punish offenses against the law of nations and (2) to declare war. In either case, there are strong constitutional grounds for taking action against terrorists. The difficulty comes in clearly identifying the enemy and being willing to risk offending many Arab nations whom we consider allies. Congress must identify the enemy and call that group a military target. Once that has happened, many of the other steps fall into place with less difficulty. It can be seen that, through diplomatic channels we must make two things very clear to the leaders of the host country. First, they should catch and punish the terrorist groups as civilian criminals.

Or, second, they should extradite the enemy soldiers to an international court for trial. If the host country fails to act on these two requests, we should make it clear that we see it as in complicity with the terrorist groups. By failing to exercise their civil responsibility, these countries leave themselves open to the consequences of allowing military forces hostile to the target government, to remain within their borders. Although diplomacy has its place, it is easy to see that diplomacy and negotiation do not strike fear in the hearts of terrorists. In most cases, diplomatic efforts have failed to bring terrorists to justice. It has been shown that Romans 13 acknowledges the government's right to bear the sword to protect its citizens from criminal threats within the country and military threats outside the country. We have also shown that military action is sanctioned by Congress to punish piracies and felonies and to punish offence against the law of nations. With these facts as background, we should now focus on the issue of just punishment. The principle here is that the punishment must be proportional to the crime. A judge could not chop off a man's hand merely because he scratched another man's hand in a fight. The punishment should be burn for burn and wound for wound. In saying this, it does not mean that the target government should not go off and start to bomb the host countries' cities if the do not do anything to stop a terrorist group that had for examples sake, kidnapped the target government's governmental officials.

However, just and proportional punishment also means that we should not apply too light a punishment. Countries that harbour terrorists and refuse to punish or extradite them should be pressured. Punishment could come in the form of economic embargoes, import-export restrictions, the serving of diplomatic relations, or even military actions. Any excessive reaction in a situation like this would not only be unjust, bit it would also fuel the fires of an even stronger retaliation from the host country. In the most desperate cases, a strike force of counterterrorists might be necessary where the threat is both real and imminent. This however, should be considered only as an option of last resort. Some examples of such actions are, in 1989, an Israeli special forces team successfully captured a man by the name of Sheik Obeid and no doubt put a dent in the terrorist network by bringing one of its leaders to justice. Another example is, in 1985, United States Air Force planes were able to force down an Egyptian airliner to prevent the escape of another terrorist leader. These are acts which should be done rarely and carefully. But, they may be appropriate means to bring about justice.

In conclusion, terrorism must be recognized as a new type of military aggression that requires governmental action. It involves an undeclared war and government officials must take the same sort of actions that they would if threatened by a hostile country. There must be changes in order to prevent further terrorist aggression in this decade and in the future. There has to be a line drawn if we are too completely eradicate this modern scourge of terrorism.

TYPES OF TERRORIST INCIDENTS

The most common types of *terrorist incidents* include:

Bombings

Bombings are the most common type of terrorist act. Typically, improvised explosive devices are inexpensive and easy to make. Modern devices are smaller and are harder to detect. They contain very destructive capabilities. Terrorists can also use materials that are readily available to the average consumer to construct a bomb.

Kidnappings and Hostage-Takings

Terrorists use kidnapping and hostage-taking to establish a bargaining position and to elicit publicity. Kidnapping is one of the most difficult acts for a terrorist group to accomplish, but, if a kidnapping is successful, it can gain terrorists money, release of jailed comrades and publicity for an extended period. Hostage-taking involves the seizure of a facility or location and the taking of hostages.

Unlike a kidnapping, hostage-taking provokes a confrontation with authorities. It forces authorities to either make dramatic decisions or to comply with the terrorist's demands. It is overt and designed to attract and hold media attention. The terrorists' intended target is the audience affected by the hostage's confinement, not the hostage.

Armed Attacks and Assassinations

Armed attacks include raids and ambushes. Assassinations are the killing of a selected victim, usually by bombings or small arms. Drive-by shootings is a common technique employed by unsophisticated or loosely organized terrorist groups. Historically, terrorists have assassinated specific individuals for psychological effect.

Arsons and Firebombings

Incendiary devices are cheap and easy to hide. Arson and firebombings are easily conducted by terrorist groups that may not be as well-organised, equipped, or trained as a major terrorist organisation. An arson or firebombing against a utility, hotel, government building, or industrial center portrays an image that the ruling government is incapable of maintaining order.

Hijackings and Skyjackings

Hijacking is the seizure by force of a surface vehicle, its passengers, and/or its cargo. Skyjacking is the taking of an aircraft, which creates a mobile, hostage barricade situation. It provides terrorists with hostages from many nations and draws heavy media attention. Skyjacking also provides mobility for the terrorists to relocate the aircraft to a country that supports their cause and provides them with a human shield, making retaliation difficult.

Other Types of Terrorist Incidents

In addition to the acts of violence discussed above, there are also numerous other types of violence that can exist under the framework of terrorism. Terrorist groups conduct maimings against their own people as a form of punishment for security violations, defections, or informing. Terrorist organizations also conduct robberies and extortion when they need to finance their acts and they don't have sponsorship from sympathetic nations. Cyberterrorism is a new form of terrorism that is everincreasing as we rely on computer networks to relay information and provide connectivity to today's modern and fast-paced world. Cyberterrorism allows terrorists to conduct their operations with little or no risk to themselves. It also provides terrorists an opportunity to disrupt or destroy networks and computers. The result is interruption of key government or business-related activities. This type of terrorism isn't as high profile as other types of terrorist attacks, but its impact is just as destructive.

Historically, terrorist attacks using nuclear, biological and chemical (NBC) weapons have been rare. Due the extremely high number of casualties that NBC weapons produce, they are also referred to as weapons of mass destruction (WMD). However, a number of nations are involved in arms races with neighbouring countries be- cause they view the development of WMD as a key de- terrent of attack by hostile neighbours. The increased development of WMD also increases the potential for terrorist groups to gain access to WMD. It is believed that in the future terrorists will have greater access to WMD because unstable nations or states may fail to safeguard their stockpiles of WMD from accidental losses, illicit sales, or outright theft or seizure. Determined terrorist groups can also gain access to WMD through covert independent research efforts or by hiring technically skilled professionals to construct the WMD.

TERRORIST GROUPS

The organizational structure of a group determines its strengths and weaknesses. A general knowledge of the prevalent models of terrorist organizations leads to a better understanding of their capabilities. Knowledge of the different labels and systems of classification that have been applied to groups and individuals aid us in discarding useless or irrelevant terms and in understanding the purposes and usefulness of different terminologies.

In recent times, the popular image of a terrorist group operating according to a specific political agenda and motivated by ideology or the desire for ethnic or national liberation dominated our understanding of terrorism. While still true of some terrorist organizations, this image is no longer universally valid. Also, a generational change in leadership of established groups is in many cases ushering in a more a destructive and relentless type of organization.

There are two general categories of organization; *hierarchical* and *networked*. The age of an organization is one of the determinants of whether it is likely to adopt a network or hierarchical structure. Newer groups tend towards organizing or adapting to the possibilities inherent in the network model. Ideology can have an effect on internal organization, with strict Leninist or Maoist groups tending towards centralized control and hierarchical structure. Within the larger structure, virtually all groups use variants of cellular organizations at the tactical level to enhance security and to task organize for operations.

Terrorist groups that are associated with a political activity or organization will often require a more hierarchical structure, in order to coordinate terrorist violence with political action. It also can be necessary for a politically affiliated group to observe "cease-fires" or avoid particular targets in support of political objectives. This can be difficult to enforce in networked organizations.

Terrorist groups can be at various stages of development in terms of capabilities and sophistication. Newer groups with fewer resources will usually be less capable and operate in permissive areas or under the tutelage of more proficient organizations to develop proficiency. Also, groups professing or associated with ethnic or nationalist agendas and limiting their operations to one country or a localized region tend to require fewer capabilities. Groups can coalesce from smaller organizations, or splinter off from larger ones.

A terrorist group may form only one cell or may form many cells that operate locally or internationally. The number of cells and their composition depend on the size of the terrorist group. A terrorist group operating within one country frequently has fewer cells and specialized teams than does an international terrorist group that may operate in several countries.

CATEGORIES OF TERRORIST GROUPS

There are many different categories of terrorism and terrorist groups that are currently in use. These categories serve to differentiate terrorist organizations according to specific criteria, which are usually related to the field or specialty of whoever is selecting the categories. Also, some categories are simply labels appended arbitrarily or redundantly, often by the media. For example, every terrorist organisation is by definition "radical", as terror tactics are not the norm for the mainstream of any group.

Separatist. Separatist groups are those with the goal of separation from existing entities through independence, political autonomy, or religious freedom or domination. The ideologies separatists subscribe to include social justice or equity, anti-imperialism, as well as the resistance to conquest or occupation by a foreign power.

Ethnocentric. Groups of this persuasion see race as the defining characteristic of a society and therefore a basis of cohesion. There is usually the attitude that a particular group is superior because of their inherent racial characteristics.

Nationalistic. The loyalty and devotion to a nation and the national consciousness derived from placing one nation's culture and interests above those of other nations or groups.

This can find expression in the creation of a new nation, or in splitting away part of an existing state to join with another that shares the perceived "national" identity.

Revolutionary. Dedicated to the overthrow of an established order and replacing it with a new political or social structure. Although often associated with communist political ideologies, this is not always the case and other political movements can advocate revolutionary methods to achieve their goals.

Political. Political ideologies are concerned with the structure and organisation of the forms of government and communities. While observers outside terrorist organizations may stress differences in political ideology, the activities of groups that are diametrically opposed on the political spectrum are similar to each other in practice.

Religious. Religiously inspired terrorism is on the rise, with a forty-three percent increase of total international terror groups espousing religious motivation between 1980 and 1995. While Islamic terrorists and organizations have been the most active and the greatest recent threat to the United States, all of the major world religions have extremists that have taken up violence to further their perceived religious goals. Religiously motivated terrorists see their objectives as holy writ and therefore infallible and non-negotiable

Social. Often particular social policies or issues will be so contentious that they will incite extremist behaviour and terrorism. Frequently this is referred to as "single issue" or "special interest" terrorism. Some issues that have produced terrorist activities in the United States and other countries include animal rights, abortion, ecology/environment and minority rights.

Domestic. These terrorists are "home-grown" and operate within and against their home country. They are frequently tied to extreme social or political factions within a particular society and focus their efforts specifically on their nation's socio-political arena.

International or Transnational. Often describing the support and operational reach of a group, these terms are often loosely defined and can be applied to widely different capabilities. *International groups* typically operate in multiple countries, but retain a geographic focus for their activities. Hezbollah has cells worldwide and has conducted operations in multiple countries, but is primarily concerned with events in Lebanon and Israel.

Transnational groups operate internationally, but are not tied to a particular country, or even region. Al Qaeda is transnational; being made up of many nationalities, having been based out of multiple countries simultaneously and conducting operations throughout the world. Their objectives affect dozens of countries with differing political systems, religions, ethnic compositions and national interests

EVOLUTION OF TERRORISM

Terrorism is continually changing. While at the surface it remains "the calculated use of unlawful violence or threat of unlawful violence to inculcate fear..." it is rapidly becoming the predominant strategic tool of our adversaries. As terrorism evolves into the principal irregular warfare strategy of the 21st century, it is adapting to changes in the world socio-political environment. Some of these changes facilitate the abilities of terrorists to operate, procure funding and develop new capabilities. Other changes are gradually moving terrorism into a different relationship with the world at large.

In order to put these changes into context, it will be necessary to look at the historical evolution of terrorism, with each succeeding evolution building upon techniques pioneered by others. This evolution is driven by ongoing developments in the nature of conflict and international relations. It is also necessary to consider some of the possible causes of future conflicts, in order to understand the actors and their motivations. Finally, we examine how terrorism will be integrated into this evolution of conflict and what that will mean for U.S. military forces.

When describing the evolution of terrorism and the use of terror through history, it is essential to remember that forms of society and government in the past were significantly different than they are today. Modern nation-states did not exist in their present form until 1648 (Treaty of Westphalia) and the state's monopoly on warfare, or inter-state violence, is even more recent. The lack of central governments made it impossible to use terror as a method of affecting a political change, as there was no single dominant political authority. Also, the absence of central authority meant that the game of warfare was open to many more players. Instead of national armies, a variety of non-sovereign nobility, mercenaries, leaders of religious factions, or mercantile companies participated in warfare. Their involvement in warfare was considered to be perfectly legitimate. This is in contrast to the modern era, where nations go to war, but private participation is actually illegal.

20th Century Evolution of Terrorism

In the early years of the 20th century nationalism and revolutionary political ideologies were the principal developmental forces acting upon terrorism. When the Treaty of Versailles redrew the map of Europe after World War I by breaking up the Austro-Hungarian Empire and creating new nations, it acknowledged the principle of self-determination for nationalities and ethnic groups. This encouraged minorities and ethnicities not receiving recognition to campaign for independence or autonomy. However, in many cases self-determination was limited to European nations and ethnic groups and denied others, especially the colonial possessions of the major European powers, creating bitterness and setting the stage for the long conflicts of the anti-colonial period.

In particular, Arab nationalists felt that they had been betrayed. Believing they were promised post-war independence, they were doubly disappointed; first when the French and British were given authority over their lands and then especially when the British allowed Zionist immigration into Palestine in keeping with a promise contained in the Balfour Declaration.

Since the end of World War II, terrorism has accelerated its development into a major component of contemporary conflict. Primarily in use immediately after the war as a subordinate element of anti-colonial insurgencies, it expanded beyond that role. In the service of various ideologies and aspirations, terrorism sometimes supplanted other forms of conflict completely. It also became a far-reaching weapon capable of effects no less global than the intercontinental bomber or missile. It has also proven to be a significant tool of diplomacy and international power for states inclined to use it.

The seemingly quick results and shocking immediacy of terrorism made some consider it as a short cut to victory. Small revolutionary groups not willing to invest the time and resources to organize political activity would rely on the "propaganda of the deed" to energize mass action. This suggested that a tiny core of activists could topple any government through the use of terror alone. The result of this belief by revolutionaries in developed countries was the isolation of the terrorists from the population they claimed to represent and the adoption of the Leninist concept of the "vanguard of revolution" by tiny groups of disaffected revolutionaries. In less developed countries small groups of foreign revolutionaries such as Che Guevara arrived from outside the country, expecting to immediately energize revolutionary action by their presence.

FUTURE TRENDS IN TERRORISM

As a conflict method that has survived and evolved through several millennia to flourish in the modern information age, terrorism continues to adapt to meet the challenges of emerging forms of conflict and exploit developments in technology and society. Terrorism has demonstrated increasing abilities to adapt to counter-terrorism measures and political failure. Terrorists are developing new capabilities of attack and improving the efficiency of existing methods. Additionally, terrorist groups have shown significant progress in escaping from a subordinate role in nation-state conflicts and becoming prominent as international influences in their own right. They are becoming more integrated with other sub-state entities, such as criminal organizations and legitimately chartered corporations and are gradually assuming a measure of control and identity with national governments.

Adaptive Capabilities of Terror Groups

Terrorists have shown the ability to adapt to the techniques and methods of counter-terror agencies and intelligence organizations over the long-term. The decentralization of the network form of organisation is an example of this. Adopted to reduce the disruption caused by the loss of key links in a chain of command, a network organisation also complicates the tasks of security forces and reduces predictability of operations.

Terrorists have also been quick to use new technologies and adapt existing ones to their uses. The debate over privacy of computer data was largely spurred by the specter of terrorists planning and communicating with encrypted data beyond law enforcement's ability to intercept or decode this data. To exchange information, terrorists have exploited disposable cellular phones, over the counter long-distance calling cards, Internet cafes and other means of anonymous communications. Embedding information in digital pictures and graphics is another innovation employed to enable the clandestine global communication that modern terrorists require.

Terrorists have also demonstrated significant resiliency after disruption by counter-terrorist action. Some groups have redefined themselves after being defeated or being forced into dormancy.

The ability to perpetuate ideology and symbology during a significant period of dormancy and re-emerge under favourable conditions demonstrates the durability of terrorism as a threat to modern societies.

Increasing Capabilities of Terrorists

Terrorists are improving their sophistication and abilities in virtually all aspects of their operations and support. The aggressive use of modern technology for information management, communication and intelligence has increased the efficiency of these activities. Weapons technology has become more increasingly available and the purchasing power of terrorist organizations is on the rise. The ready availability of both technology and trained personnel to operate it for any client with sufficient cash allows the well-funded terrorist to equal or exceed the sophistication of governmental countermeasures.

Likewise, due to the increase in information outlets and competition with increasing numbers of other messages, terrorism now requires a greatly increased amount of violence or novelty to attract the attention it requires. The tendency of major media to compete for ratings and the subsequent revenue realized from increases in their audience size and share produces pressures on terrorists to increase the impact and violence of their actions to take advantage of this sensationalism.

Today, most experts believe that certain parts of the Middle East, Pakistan and Afghanistan are turning out to be the main power centres for terrorism. Decades of lawlessness and corruption have seen Islamic terrorist groups fill the power vaccum in this region and continue to turn out an alarming number of religiously motivated terrorists.

5

State Terrorism and Comprehensive Conventions

State terrorism refers to acts of terrorism conducted by governments. Like the definitions of "terrorism" and "state-sponsored terrorism", the definition of "state terrorism" remains controversial and without international consensus.

Scholar Gus Martin describes state terrorism as terrorism "committed by governments and quasi-governmental agencies and personnel against perceived enemies," which can be directed against both domestic and external enemies. The original general meaning of terrorism was of terrorism by the state, as reflected in the 1798 supplement of the Dictionnaire of the Academie Francaise, which described terrorism as *systeme, regime de la terreur*. Similarly, a terrorist in the late 18th century was considered any person "who attempted to further his views by a system of coercive intimidation." The terms "establishment terrorism," "terrorism from above" (as opposed to "terrorism from below" (terrorism by non-state groups) and "structural terrorism" are sometimes used to denote state terrorism.

The Encyclopaedia Britannica Online defines terrorism generally as "the systematic use of violence to create a general climate of fear in a population and thereby to bring about a particular political objective," and adds that terrorism has been practiced by "state institutions such as armies, intelligence services and police." The encyclopedia adds that "stablishment terrorism, often called state or state-sponsored terrorism, is employed by governments — or more often by factions within governments — against that government's citizens, against factions within the government, or against foreign governments or groups."

While the most common modern usage of the word terrorism refers to civilian-victimizing political violence by insurgents or conspirators, scholars typically make a broader interpretation of the nature of terrorism that encompasses the concepts of state terrorism and state-sponsored terrorism. In fact, terrorism scholar Michael Stohl argues, "The use of terror tactics is common in international relations and the state has been and remains a more likely employer of terrorism within the international system than insurgents. Stohl clarifies, however, that "of all acts of state violence are terrorism. It is important to understand that in terrorism the violence threatened or perpetrated, has purposes broader than simple physical harm to a victim. The audience of the act or threat of violence is more important than the immediate victim."

History

Terror by states has a long history. For example, Aristotle wrote critically of terror employed by tyrants against their subjects. The earliest use of the word *terrorism* identified by the *Oxford English Dictionary* is a 1795 reference to tyrannical state behaviour, the "reign of terrorism" in France. In that same year, Edmund Burke famously decried the "thousands of those hell-hounds called terrorists" who he believed threatened Europe. During the Reign of Terror, the Jacobin government and other factions of the French Revolution used the apparatus of the state to execute and intimidate political opponents and the Oxford English Dictionary includes as one definition of terrorism "Government by intimidation carried out by the party in power in France between 1789-1794".

Later exemplars of state terrorism were the police state measures employed by the Soviet Union beginning in the

1920s and by Germany's Nazi regime in the 1930s and 1940s. The bombing of Guernica has been called an act of terrorism and other examples of state terrorism may include the World War II bombings of London, Dresden and Hiroshima and the Japanese sneak attack on the U.S. Naval Base at Pearl Harbor, Hawaii.

The state of Israel were among other incidents accused of state terrorism regarding the unlawful boarding and killing of 10 people on the Ship to gaza flotilla. Claims that this is state terrorism was made by the Iranian president Mahmoud Ahmadinejad and Turkish Prime Minister Tayyip Erdogan.

Scholars Michael Stohl and George A. Lopez argue that an institutionalized form of terrorism carried out by states has occurred as a result of changes taking place following World War ll. In this analysis, state terrorism as a form of foreign policy was shaped by the presence and use of weapons of mass destruction and that the legitimizing of such violent behaviour led to increasing acceptance, when it was employed by states, of violence that had earlier been labelled terrorist.

Types

Stolhl and George A. Lopez designate three particular forms of state terrorism exhibited in foreign policy behaviour:

1. **Coercive terrorist diplomacy**: (e.g. discreet and controlled and makes non-compliance intolerable)
2. **Covert state terrorism**:
   - *(a) Clandestine state terrorism* (e.g. direct participation of states, ex. to weaken a governments or intimidate government officials of another state etc.)
   - *(b) State-sponsored terrorism* (e.g. "states or private groups being employed to undertake terrorist actions on behalf of sponsoring state."

3. **Surrogate terrorism**: (e.g. assistance to another state or group that improves their capability to practice terrorism)

   (a) *State-sponsored terrorism* (e.g. as above)

   (b) *State acquiescence to terrorism* (e.g. group undertakes terrorism and is not explicitly backed by a state but not condemned either.)

Combatting State Terrorism

In *Understanding Terrorism: Challenges, Perspectives and Issues,* Gus Martin argues that the work of organizations such as Human Rights Watch and Amnesty International are among the "approaches to the analyses of state terrorism [that] are useful for evaluating different types of state-sponsored violence," arguing further that during the late 1970s and 80's "in its annual global human rights reports Amnesty International has extensively documented the escalation in state terror...Amnesty International identified the main forms of state terror as arbitrary detention, unfair trial, torture and political murder or extrajudicial execution."

Moral Analysis

Philosopher Igor Primoratz provides four reasons why he believes that state terrorism is typically morally worse than non-state terrorism. First, because of the nature of the modern state and "the amount and variety of resources" available even for small states, the state mode of terrorism claims vastly more victims than does terrorism by non-state actors. Secondly, because "state terrorism is bound to be compounded by secrecy, deception and hypocrisy," terrorist states typically act with clandestine brutality while publicly professing adherence to "values and principles which rule it out." Thirdly, because unlike non-state actors, states are signatories in international laws and conventions prohibiting terrorism, so when a state commits acts of terrorism it is "in breach of its own solemn international commitments." Finally, while there may be circumstances where non-state actors are in such an oppressed situation that there may be no alternative but terrorism, Primoratz argues that "it seems virtually impossible that a state should find itself in such circumstances where it has no alternative to resorting to terrorism."

Arguments that States are Incapable of Terrorism

In recent decades the term terrorism has more often been applied to violent non-state actors and some scholars dispute whether the concept of terrorism is properly applied to states.

So far without success, the United Nations has attempted to create an international legal definition of terrorism that excludes state terrorism. The Chairman of the United Nations Counter-Terrorism Committee has stated that the twelve previous international conventions on terrorism had never referred to state terrorism, which was not an international legal concept and that when states abuse their powers they should be judged against international conventions dealing with war crimes, international human rights and international humanitarian law, rather than against international anti-terrorism statutes. In a similar vein, Kofi Annan, at the time United Nations Secretary-General, stated that it is "time to set aside debates on so-called 'state terrorism'. The use of force by states is already regulated under international law" Annan added, "...regardless of the differences between governments on the question of definition of terrorism, what is clear and what we can all agree on is any deliberate attack on innocent civilians, regardless of one's cause, is unacceptable and fits into the definition of terrorism."

Various analysts have attempted to formulate terrorism definitions that are neutral with respect to the perpetrators of the act, thus permitting a definition's logically consistent application to both non-state and state actors. However, perhaps in contrast, a recent unofficial definition of the word published by the United Nations states that "Terrorism is an anxiety-inspiring method of repeated violent action, employed by (semi-) clandestine individual, group or state actors, for idiosyncratic, criminal or political reasons, whereby — in contrast to assassination — the direct targets of violence are not the main targets. The immediate human victims of violence are generally chosen randomly (targets of opportunity) or selectively (representative or symbolic targets) from a target population and serve as message generators. Threat- and violence-based communication processes between terrorist (organisation), (imperiled) victims and main targets are used to manipulate the main target (audience(s)), turning it into a target of terror, a target of demands, or a target of attention, depending on whether intimidation, coercion, or propaganda is primarily sought."

Noam Chomsky and Edward S. Herman, described as pioneers in late twentieth century thinking about state terrorism, have argued that the distinction between state and non-state terror is morally relativist and distracts from or justifies state terrorism perpetrated by favored states, typically those of wealthy and developed nations. Chomsky has described low-intensity warfare as state terrorism and writes: "The U.S. is officially committed to what is called 'low-intensity warfare'.... If you read the definition of low-intensity conflict in army manuals and compare it with official definitions of 'terrorism' in army manuals, or the U.S. Code, you find they're almost the same."

The **definition of terrorism** has proved controversial. Various legal systems and government agencies use different definitions of "terrorism". Moreover, the International community has been slow to formulate a universally agreed, legally binding definition of this crime. These difficulties arise from the fact that the term "terrorism" is politically and emotionally charged.

The Sectoral Approach

In order to elaborate an effective legal regime to prevent and punish international terrorism, rather than only working on a single, all-encompasing, comprehensive definition of terrorism, the international community has also adopted a "'sectoral' approach aimed at identifying offences seen as belonging to the activities of terrorists and working out treaties in order to deal with specific categories thereof". The treaties that follow this approach focus on the wrongful nature of terrorist activities rather than on their intent:

On the whole, therefore, the 'sectoral' conventions confirm the assumption that some offences can be considered *in themselves* as offences of international concern, irrespective of any 'terrorist' intent or purpose. Indeed, the principal merit of the 'sectoral approach' is that it avoids the need to define 'terrorism' of 'terrorist acts' (...) So long as the 'sectoral' approach is followed, there is no need to define terrorism; a definition would only be necessary if the punishment of the relevant offences were made conditional on the existance of a specific 'terrorist' intent; but this would be counter-productive, inasmuch as it would result in unduly restricting their suppression.

Following this approach, the international community has adopted the following sectoral counter-terrorism conventions, open to the ratification of all states:

- The 1963 Convention on Offences and Certain Other Acts Committed On Board Aircraft
- The 1970 Convention for the Suppression of Unlawful Seizure of Aircraft

- The 1971 Convention for the Suppression of Unlawful Acts Against the Safety of Civil Aviation
- The 1979 Convention on the Physical Protection of Nuclear Material
- The 1988 Protocol for the Suppression of Unlawful Acts of Violence at Airports Serving International Civil Aviation
- The 1988 Convention for the Suppression of Unlawful Acts Against the Safety of Maritime Navigation
- The 1988 Protocol for the Suppression of Unlawful Acts Against the Safety of Fixed Platforms Located on the Continental Shelf
- The 1991 Convention on the Marking of Plastic Explosives for the Purpose of Identification
- The 1997 International Convention for the Suppression of Terrorist Bombings.
- The 1999 International Convention for the Suppression of the Financing of Terrorism
- The 2005 International Convention for the Suppression of Acts of Nuclear Terrorism

Analyzing these treaties, Andrew Byrnes observed that:

These conventions — all of which are described by the United Nations as part of its panoply of anti-terrorist measures – share three principal characteristics:

(a) they all adopted an "operational definition" of a specific type of terrorist act that was defined without reference to the underlying political or ideological purpose or motivation of the perpetrator of the act — this reflected a consensus that there were some acts

that were such a serious threat to the interests of all that they could not be justified by reference to such motives;

(b) they all focused on actions by non-State actors (individuals and organisations) and the State was seen as an active ally in the struggle against terrorism – the question of the State itself as terrorist actor was left largely to one side; and

(c) they all adopted a criminal law enforcement model to address the problem, under which States would cooperate in the apprehension and prosecution of those alleged to have committed these crimes.

Byrnes notes that "this act-specific approach to addressing problems of terrorism in binding international treaties has continued up until relatively recently. Although political denunciation of terrorism in all its forms had continued apace, there had been no successful attempt to define 'terrorism' as such in a broad sense that was satisfactory for legal purposes. There was also some scepticism as to the necessity, desirability and feasibility of producing an agreed and workable general definition." Nonetheless, since 2000, the United Nations General Assembly has been working on a proposed Comprehensive Convention on International Terrorism.

Comprehensive Conventions

The international community has worked on two comprehensive counter-terrorism treaties, the League of Nations' 1937 Convention for the prevention and punishment of Terrorism, that never entered into force and the proposed Comprehensive Convention on International Terrorism, that has not been finalized yet.

Proposed Comprehensive Convention on International Terrorism

Since 2000, the United Nations General Assembly has been negotiating a Comprehensive Convention on International Terrorism. The definition of the crime of terrorism, which has been on the negotiating table since 2002 reads as follows:

"1. Any person commits an offence within the meaning of this Convention if that person, by any means, unlawfully and intentionally, causes:

(a) Death or serious bodily injury to any person; or

(b) Serious damage to public or private property, including a place of public use, a State or government facility, a public transportation system, an infrastructure facility or the environment; or

(c) Damage to property, places, facilities, or systems referred to in paragraph 1 (b) of this article, resulting or likely to result in major economic loss, when the purpose of the conduct, by its nature or context, is to intimidate a population, or to compel a Government or an international organisation to do or abstain from doing any act."

That definition is not controversial in itself; the deadlock in the negotiations arises instead from the opposing views on whether such a definition would be applicable to the armed forces of a state and to Self-determination movements. Thalif Deen described the situation as follows: "The key sticking points in the draft treaty revolve around several controversial yet basic issues, including the definition of ´terrorism´. For example, what distinguishes a "terrorist organization" from a 'liberation movement'? And do you exclude activities of national armed forces, even if they are perceived to commit acts of terrorism? If not, how much of this constitutes 'state terrorism'?" The coordinator of the negotiations, supported by most western delegations, proposed the following exceptions to address those issues:

> "1. Nothing in this Convention shall affect other rights, obligations and responsibilities of States, peoples and individuals under international law, in particular the purposes and principles of the Charter of the United Nations and international humanitarian law.
>
> 2. The activities of **armed forces** during an armed conflict, as those terms are understood under international humanitarian law, which are governed by that law, are not governed by this Convention.
>
> 3. The activities undertaken by the military forces of a State in the exercise of their official duties, **inasmuch as they are governed** by other rules of international law, are not governed by this Convention.
>
> 4. Nothing in this article condones or makes lawful otherwise unlawful acts, nor precludes prosecution under other laws."

The state members of the Organization of the Islamic Conference proposed instead the following exceptions:

> "2. The activities of **the parties** during an armed conflict, **including in situations of foreign occupation**, as those terms are understood under international humanitarian law, which are governed by that law, are not governed by this Convention.
>
> 3. The activities undertaken by the military forces of a State in the exercise of their official duties, **inasmuch as they are in conformity** with international law, are not governed by this Convention."

Sectoral Conventions

The various sectoral counter-terrorism conventions define and criminalized particular categories of terrorist activities.

Terrorist Bombings Convention

Article 2.1 of the 1997 International Convention for the Suppression of Terrorist Bombings defines the offence of terrorist bombing as follows:

> "Any person commits an offence within the meaning of this Convention if that person unlawfully and intentionally delivers, places, discharges or detonates an explosive or other lethal device in, into or against a place or public use, a State or government facility, a public transportation system or an infrastructure facility:
>
> (a) With the intent to cause death or serious bodily injury; or
>
> (b) With the intent to cause extensive destruction of such a place, facility or system, where such a destruction results in or is likely to result in major economic loss.

Article 19 expressly excluded from the scope of the convention certain activities of state armed forces and of self-determination movements as follows:

> "1. Nothing in this Convention shall affect other rights, obligations and responsibilities of States and individuals under international law, in particular the purposes and principles of the Charter of the United Nations and international humanitarian law.
>
> 2. The activities of armed forces during an armed conflict, as those terms are understood under international humanitarian law, which are governed by that law, are not governed by this Convention and the activities

undertaken by the military forces of a State in the exercise of their official duties, inasmuch as they are governed by other rules of international law, are not governed by this Convention."

Terrorist Financing Convention

Article 2.1 of the 1999 sectoral United Nations International Convention for the Suppression of the Financing of Terrorism (Terrorist Financing Convention) defines the crime of terrorist financing as the offence committed by "any person" who "by any means, directly or indirectly, unlawfully and wilfully, provides or collects funds with the intention that they should be used or in the knowledge that they are to be used, in full or in part, in order to carry out" an act "intended to cause death or serious bodily injury to a civilian, or to any other person not taking an active part in the hostilities in a situation of armed conflict, when the purpose of such act, by its nature or context, is to intimidate a population, or to compel a government or an international organisation to do or to abstain from doing any act."

Nuclear Terrorism Convention

The 2005 United Nations International Convention for the Suppression of Acts of Nuclear Terrorism defines the crime of nuclear terrorism as follows:

Article 2

1. Any person commits an offence within the meaning of this Convention if that person unlawfully and intentionally: (a) Possesses radioactive material or makes or possesses a device:

(i) With the intent to cause death or serious bodily injury; or

(ii) With the intent to cause substantial damage to property or to the environment;

(b) Uses in any way radioactive material or a device, or uses or damages a nuclear facility in a manner which releases or risks the release of radioactive material:

(i) With the intent to cause death or serious bodily injury; or

(ii) With the intent to cause substantial damage to property or to the environment; or

(iii) With the intent to compel a natural or legal person, an international organisation or a State to do or refrain from doing an act.

Article 4 of the convention expressly excluded from the application of the convention the use of nuclear weapons during armed conflicts without, though, recognizing the legality of the use of those weapons:

1. Nothing in this Convention shall affect other rights, obligations and responsibilities of States and individuals under international law, in particular the purposes and principles of the Charter of the United Nations and international humanitarian law.

2. The activities of armed forces during an armed conflict, as those terms are understood under international humanitarian law, which are governed by that law are not governed by this Convention and the activities undertaken by military forces of a State in the exercise of their official duties, inasmuch as they are governed by other rules of international law, are not governed by this Convention.

3. The provisions of paragraph 2 of the present article shall not be interpreted as condoning or making lawful

otherwise unlawful acts, or precluding prosecution under other laws.

4. This Convention does not address, nor can it be interpreted as addressing, in any way, the issue of the legality of the use or threat of use of nuclear weapons by States.

Definitions of Terrorism in Other UN Decisions

In parallel with the criminal law codification efforts, some United Nations organs have put forward some broad political definitions of terrorism.

UN General Assembly Resolutions

On December 17, 1996, the non-binding United Nations Declaration to Supplement the 1994 Declaration on Measures to Eliminate International Terrorism, annexed to the UN General Assembly Resolution 51/210, condemned terrorist activities in the following terms:

"1. The States Members of the United Nations solemnly reaffirm their unequivocal condemnation of all acts, methods and practices of terrorism as criminal and unjustifiable, wherever and by whomsoever committed, including those that jeopardize friendly relations among States and peoples and threaten the territorial integrity and security of States;

2. The States Members of the United Nations reaffirm that acts, methods and practices of terrorism are contrary to the purposes and principles of the United Nations; they declare that knowingly financing, planning and inciting terrorist acts are also contrary to the purposes and principles of the United Nations;"

3. Criminal acts intended or calculated to provoke a state of terror in the general public, a group of persons or

> particular persons for political purposes are in any circumstance unjustifiable, whatever the considerations of a political, philosophical, ideological, racial, ethnic, religious or any other nature that may be invoked to justify them;"

Antonio Cassese has argued that the language contained in these declarations "sets out an acceptable definition of terrorism."

UN Security Council

In 2004, United Nations Security Council Resolution 1566 condemned terrorist acts as:

> "criminal acts, including against civilians, committed with the intent to cause death or serious bodily injury, or taking of hostages, with the purpose to provoke a state of terror in the general public or in a group of persons or particular persons, intimidate a population or compel a government or an international organisation to do or to abstain from doing any act, which constitute offences within the scope of and as defined in the international conventions and protocols relating to terrorism, are under no circumstances justifiable by considerations of a political, philosophical, ideological, racial, ethnic, religious or other similar nature,"

The High-Level Panel on Threats, Challenges and Change and the Secretary General

Also in 2004, a High-Level Panel on Threats, Challenges and Change composed of independent experts and convened by the Secretary-General of the United Nations called states to set aside their differences and to adopt, in the text of a proposed Comprehensive Convention on International Terrorism, the following political "description of terrorism":

> "any action, in addition to actions already specified by the existing conventions on aspects of terrorism, the Geneva Conventions and Security Council resolution 1566 (2004), that is intended to cause death or serious bodily harm to civilians or non-combatants, when the purpose of such an act, by its nature or context, is to intimidate a population, or to compel a Government or an international organisation to do or to abstain from doing any act."

The following year, the then Secretary-General of the United Nations Kofi Annan endorsed the High Level Panel's definition of terrorism and asked states to set aside their differences and to adopt that definition within the proposed comprehensive terrorism convention before the end of that year. He said:

> "It is time to set aside debates on so-called "State terrorism". The use of force by states is already thoroughly regulated under international law. And the right to resist occupation must be understood in its true meaning. It cannot include the right to deliberately kill or maim civilians. I endorse fully the High-level Panel's call for a definition of terrorism, which would make it clear that, in addition to actions already proscribed by existing conventions, any action constitutes terrorism if it is intended to cause death or serious bodily harm to civilians or non-combatants with the purpose of intimidating a population or compelling a Government or an international organisation to do or abstain from doing any act. I believe this proposal has clear moral force and I strongly urge world leaders to unite behind it and to conclude a comprehensive convention on terrorism before the end of the sixtieth session of the General Assembly."

The suggestion of incorporating such a political definition of terrorism into the comprehensive convention was rejected. United Nations' member states noted that a political definition such as the one proposed by the High-Level Panel on Threats, Challenges and Change and endorsed by the Secteray General, lacked the necessary requirements to be incorporated in a criminal law instrument. Carlos Diaz-Paniagua, who coordinated the negotiations of the proposed Comprehensive Convention on International Terrorism, stated that a comprehensive definition of terrorism to be included in a criminal law treaty must have "legal precision, certainty and fair-labeling of the criminal conduct - all of which emanate from the basic human rights obligation to observe due process."

●●

6
Terrorism in India

Terrorism in India is primarily attributable some religious communities and Naxalite radical movements. The regions with long-term terrorist activities today are Jammu and Kashmir, Mumbai, Central India (Naxalism) and Seven Sister States (independence and autonomy movements). In the past, the Punjab insurgency led to militant activities in the Indian state of Punjab as well as the national capital Delhi.

As of 2006, at least 232 of the country's 608 districts were afflicted, at differing intensities, by various insurgent and terrorist movements. In August 2008, National Security Advisor M K Narayanan has said that there are as many as 800 terrorist cells operating in the country.

CHRONOLOGY OF MAJOR INCIDENTS

Western India

Maharashtra

Mumbai has been the most preferred target for most terrorist organizations, primarily the separatist forces from Pakistan. Over the past few years a series of attacks including explosions in local trains in July 2006, to the most recent and unprecedented attacks of 26 November 2008, where two of the prime hotels, a landmark train station and a Jewish Chabad house, in south Mumbai, were attacked and sieged. Terrorist attacks in Mumbai include:

- 12 March 1993 - Series of 13 bombs go off killing 257
- 6 December 2002 - Bomb goes off in a bus in Ghatkopar killing 2

- 27 January 2003 - Bomb goes off on a bicycle in Vile Parle killing 1
- 14 March 2003 - Bomb goes off in a train in Mulund killing 10
- 28 July 2003 - Bomb goes off in a bus in Ghatkopar killing 4
- 25 August 2003 - Two Bombs go off in cars near the Gateway of India and Zaveri Bazaar killing 50
- 11 July 2006 - Series of seven bombs go off in trains killing 209
- 26 November 2008 to 29 November 2008 - Coordinated series of attacks killing at least 172.

On 13 February 2010, a bomb explosion at the German Bakery in Pune killed fourteen people and injured at least 60 more.

Northern and Northwestern India

Bihar

Existence of certain insurgent groups like the *CPI-ML, Peoples War Group* and *MCC,* is a major concern as they frequently attack local policemen and politicians.

Poor governance and the law and order system in Bihar have helped increase the menace caused by the militias.

The State has witnessed many massacres by these groups. The main victims of the violence by these groups are helpless people (including women, old and children) who are killed in massacres. The state police is ill equipped to take on the AK-47, AK-56 of the militants with their vintage 303 rifles. The militants have used landmines to kill ambush police parties as well.

The root cause of the militant activities in the state is huge disparity among different caste groups. After Independence, land reforms were supposed to be implemented, thereby giving the low caste and the poor a share in the lands which was till then held mostly by high caste people.

However, due to caste based divisive politics in the state land reforms were never implemented properly. This led to growing sense of alienation among the low caste.

Communist groups like CPI-ML, MCC and People's War Group took advantage of this and instigated the low caste people to take up arms against establishment which was seen as a tool in the hands of rich. They started taking up lands of rich by force killing the high caste people.

The high caste people resorted to use of force by forming their own army *Ranvir Sena* to take on the naxalites. The State witnessed a bloody period in which the groups tried to prove their supremacy by mass killings. The Police remained a mute witness to these killings as it lacked the means to take any action.

However, now the Ranvir Sena has significantly weakened with the arrest of its top brass. The other groups are still active.

There have been arrests in various parts of the country, particularly those made by the Delhi and Mumbai police in the recent past, indicating that extremist/terrorist outfits have been spreading their networks in this State. There is a strong suspicion that Bihar is also being used as a transit point by the small-arms, fake currency and drug dealers entering from Nepal and terrorists reportedly infiltrating through Nepal and Bangladesh.

However, in recent years these attacks by various caste groups have come down with better government being practised.

Punjab

During 1970s, the Indian Green Revolution brought increased economic prosperity for the Sikh community in Punjab. This propensity kindled an age old fear in the Sikh community — that of being absorbed into the Hindu fold - and led to the rise of Sikh militants.

The insurgency intensified during 1980s when the movement turned violent and the name Khalistan resurfaced and sought independence from the Indian Union. Led by Jarnail Singh Bhindranwale who, though not in favour in the creation of Khalistan but also was not against it, began using militancy to stress the movement's demands. Soon things turned bloody with India alleging that neighbouring Pakistan supported these militants, who, by 1983-84, had begun to enjoy widespread support among Sikhs.

In 1984, Operation Blue Star was conducted by the Indian government to stem out the movement. It involved an assault on the Golden Temple complex, which Sant Bhindranwale had fortifed in preparation of an army assault. Indira Gandhi, India's then Prime Minister, ordered the military to storm the temple, who eventually had to use tanks.

After a seventy-four-hour firefight, the army successfully took control of the temple. In doing so, it damaged some portions of the Akal Takht, the Sikh Reference Library and some damaged to the Golden Temple itself. According to Indian government sources, eighty-three army personnel were killed and 249 injured. Militant casualties were 493 killed and eighty-six injured.

During same year, the assassination of Indira Gandhi by two Sikh bodyguards, believed to be driven by the Golden Temple affair, resulted in widespread anti-Sikh riots, especially in New Delhi. Following Operation Black Thunder in 1988,

Punjab Police, first under Julio Ribeiro and then under KPS Gill, together with the Indian Army eventually succeeded in pushing the movement underground. In 1985, Sikh terrorists bombed an Air India flight from Canada to India, killing all 329 people on board. It is the worst terrorist act in Canada's history.

The ending of Sikh militancy and the desire for a Khalistan catalyzed when the then-Prime Minister of Pakistan, Benazir Bhutto handed all intelligence material concerning Punjab militancy to the Indian government, as a goodwill gesture. The Indian government used that intelligence to put an end to those who were behind attacks in India and militancy.

The ending of overt Sikh militancy in 1993 led to a period of relative calm, punctuated by militant acts (*i.e.* the assassination of Punjab CM, Beant Singh in 1995) attributed to half a dozen or so operating Sikh militant organisations. These organizations include Babbar Khalsa International, Khalistan Commando Force, Khalistan Liberation Force and Khalistan Zindabad Force.

New Delhi

Three explosions went off in the Indian capital of New Delhi on 29 October 2005 which killed more than 60 people and injured at least 200 others. The high number of casualties made the bombings the deadliest attack in India of 2005.It was followed by 5 bomb blasts on 13 September 2008.

Attack on Indian Parliament

Terrorists on 13 December 2001 attacked the Parliament of India resulting in a 45-minute gun battle in which 9 policemen and parliament staffer were killed. All the five terrorists were also killed by the security forces and were identified as Pakistani nationals. The attack took place around 11:40 am (IST), minutes after both Houses of Parliament had adjourned for the day.

The suspected terrorists dressed in commando fatigues entered Parliament in a car through the VIP gate of the building. Displaying Parliament and Home Ministry security stickers, the vehicle entered the Parliament premises.

The terrorists set off massive blasts and used AK-47 rifles, explosives and grenades for the attack. Senior Ministers and over 200 Members of Parliament were inside the Central Hall of Parliament when the attack took place. Security personnel sealed the entire premises which saved many lives.

Uttar Pradesh

Ayodhya Crisis

The long simmering Ayodhya crisis finally culminated in a terrorist attack on the site of the 16th century Babri Masjid — Demolished Ancient Masjid in Ayodhya on 5 July 2005. Following the two-hour gunfight between Lashkar-e-Toiba terrorists based in Pakistan and Indian police, in which six terrorists were killed, opposition parties called for a nationwide strike with the country's leaders condemning the attack, believed to have been masterminded by Dawood Ibrahim.

Varanasi Blasts

A series of blasts occurred across the Hindu holy city of Varanasi on 7 March 2006. Fifteen people are reported to have been killed and as many as 101 others were injured. No-one has accepted responsibility for the attacks, but it is speculated that the bombings were carried out in retaliation of the arrest of a Lashkar-e-Toiba agent in Varanasi earlier in February 2006.

On 5 April 2006 the Indian police arrested six Islamic militants, including a cleric who helped plan bomb blasts. The cleric is believed to be a commander of a banned Bangladeshi Islamic militant group, Harkatul Jihad-al Islami and is linked to the Inter-Services Intelligence, the Pakistani spy agency.

Northeastern India

Northeastern India consists 7 states (also known as *the seven sisters*): Assam, Meghalaya, Tripura, Arunachal Pradesh, Mizoram, Manipur and Nagaland. Tensions exists between these states and the central government as well as amongst the tribal people, who are natives of these states and migrant peoples from other parts of India.

The states have accused New Delhi of ignoring the issues concerning them. It is this feeling which has led the natives of these states to seek greater participation in self-governance. There are existing territorial disputes between Manipur and Nagaland.

There is a rise of insurgent activities and regional movements in the northeast, especially in the states of Assam, Nagaland, Mizoram and Tripura. Most of these organizations demand independent state status or increased regional autonomy and sovereignty.

North Eastern region tension have eased off-late with Indian and state government's concerted effort to raise the living standards of the people in these regions. However, militancy still exists in this region of India supported by external sources.

Nagaland

The first and perhaps the most significant insurgency was in Nagaland from the early 1950s until it was finally quelled in the early 1980s through a mixture of repression and co-optation. The *National Socialist Council of Nagaland-Isak-Muivah* (NSCN-IM), demands an independent Nagaland and has carried out several attacks on Indian military installations in the region. According to government officials,

599 civilians, 235 security forces and 862 terrorists have lost their lives between 1992 and 2000.

On 14 June 2001, a cease-fire agreement was signed between the Government of India and the NSCN-IM which had received widespread approval and support in Nagaland. Terrorist outfits such as the Naga National Council-Federal (NNC-F) and the National Council of Nagaland-Khaplang (NSCN-K) also welcomed the development.

Certain neighbouring states, especially Manipur, raised serious concerns over the cease-fire. They feared that NSCN would continue insurgent activities in its state and demanded New Delhi scrap the ceasefire deal and renew military action. Despite the cease-fire the NSCN has continued its insurgency.

Assam

After Nagaland, Assam is the most volatile state in the region. Beginning 1979, the indigenous people of Assam demanded that the illegal immigrants who had emigrated from Bangladesh to Assam be detected and deported. The movement lead by All Assam Students Union began non-violently with satyagraha, boycotts, picketing and courting arrests.

Those protesting frequently came under police action. In 1983 an election was conducted which was opposed by the movement leaders. The election lead to widespread violence. The movement finally ended after the movement leaders signed an agreement (called Assam Accord) with the central government in 15 August 1985.

Under the provisions of this accord, anyone who entered the state illegally between January 1966 and March 1971 were allowed to remain but were disenfranchised for ten years, while those who entered after 1971 faced expulsion. A November 1985 amendment to the Indian citizenship law allows non-citizens who entered Assam between 1961 and

1971 to have all the rights of citizenship except the right to vote for a period of ten years.

New Delhi also gave special administration autonomy to the Bodos in the state. However, the Bodos demanded for a separate Bodoland which led to a clash between the Bengalis, the Bodos and the Indian military resulting in hundreds of deaths.

There are several organizations which advocate the independence of Assam. The most prominent of which is the ULFA (United Liberation Front of Assam). Formed in 1971, the ULFA has two main goals, the independence of Assam and the establishment of a socialist government.

The ULFA has carried out several terrorist attacks in the region targeting the Indian Military and non-combatants. The group assassinates political opponents, attacks police and other security forces, blasts railroad tracks and attacks other infrastructure facilities. The ULFA is believed to have strong links with *Nationalist Socialist Council of Nagaland (NSCN)*, Maoists and the Naxalites.

It is also believed that they carry out most of their operations from the Kingdom of Bhutan. Because of ULFA's increased visibility, the Indian government outlawed the group in 1986 and declared Assam a troubled area. Under pressure from New Delhi, Bhutan carried a massive operation to drive out the ULFA militants from its territory.

Backed by the Indian Army, Thimphu was successful in killing more than a thousand terrorists and extraditing many more to India while sustaining only 120 casualties. The Indian military undertook several successful operations aimed at countering future ULFA terrorist attacks, but the ULFA continues to be active in the region. In 2004, the ULFA targeted a public school in Assam killing 19 children and 5 adults.

Assam remains the only state in the northeast where terrorism is still a major issue. The Indian Military was successful in dismantling terrorist outfits in other areas, but have been criticized by human rights groups for allegedly using harsh methods when dealing with terrorists.

Tripura

Tripura witnessed a surge in terrorist activities in the 1990s. New Delhi blamed Bangladesh for providing a safe haven to the insurgents operating from its territory. The area under control of the *Tripura Tribal Areas Autonomous District Council* was increased after a tripartite agreement between New Delhi, the state government of Tripura and the Council. The government has since been brought the movement under control though certain rebellious factions still linger.

Manipur

In Manipur, militants formed an organization known as the *People's Liberation Army*. Their main goal was to unite the Meitei tribes of Burma and establish an independent state of Manipur. However, the movement was thought to have been suppressed after a fierce clash with Indian security forces in the mid-1990s.

On 18 September 2005, six separatist rebels were killed in fighting between Zomi Revolutionary Army and Zomi Revolutionary Front in the Churachandpur District.

On 20 September 2005, 14 Indian soldiers were ambushed and killed by 20 rebels from the Kanglei Yawol Kanna Lup (KYKL) terrorist organisation, armed with AK-56 rifles, in the village of Nariang, 22 miles southwest of Manipur's capital Imphal. "Unidentified rebels using automatic weapons ambushed a road patrol of the army's Gorkha Rifles killing eight on the spot," said a spokesman for the Indian government.

Mizoram

The *Mizo National Front* fought for over two decades with the Indian Military in an effort to gain independence. As in neighbouring states the insurgency was quelled by force.

South India

Karnataka

Karnataka is considerably less affected by terrorism in spite of having many places of historical importance and the IT hub of India, Bengaluru. However, recently Naxal activity has been increasing in the Western Ghats. Also, a few attacks have occurred, major ones including an attack on IISc on 28 December 2005 and serial blasts in Bengaluru on 26 July 2008.

Andhra Pradesh

Andhra Pradesh is one of the few southern states affected by terrorism, although of a far different kind and on a much smaller scale. The terrorism in Andhra Pradesh stems from the *People's War Group* (PWG), popularly known as Naxalites.

The 'PWG, has been operating in India for over two decades with most of its operations in the Telangana region in Andhra Pradesh. The group is also active in Orissa and Bihar. Unlike the Kashmiri insurgents and ULFA, PWG is a Maoist terrorist organization and communism is one of its primary goals.

Having failed to capture popular support in the elections, they resorted to violence as a means to voice their opinions. The group targets Indian Police, multinational companies and other influential institutions in the name of the communism. PWG has also targeted senior government officials, including the attempted assassination of former Andhra Pradesh Chief Minister Chandrababu Naidu.

It reportedly has a strength of 800 to 1,000 well armed militiants and is believed to have close links with the Maoists in Nepal and the LTTE of Sri Lanka. According to the Indian government, on an average, more than 60 civilians, 60 naxal rebels and a dozen policemen are killed every year because of PWG led insurgency. Also one of the major terrorist attack is 25 August 2007 Hyderabad Bombing.

Tamil Nadu

Tamil Nadu had (LTTE) *Liberation Tigers of Tamil Eelam* militants operating in state Tamil Nadu up until the assassination of former Prime Minister Rajiv Gandhi. LTTE had given many speeches in state Tamil Nadu led by Velupillai Prabhakaran, Tamilselvan and other Eelam members. Tamil Tigers, now a banned organization, have been receiving many donations and support from India in the past. The Tamil Nadu Liberation Army, a militant Tamil movement in India that have ties to LTTE. Tamil Nadu also faced terrorist attacks orchestrated by Muslim funadamentalists. For more information refer, 1998 Coimbatore bombings.

7
Insurgency in Jammu and Kashmir

Insurgency in Kashmir has existed in various forms, both on the Indian administrated side of the disputed territory of Jammu and Kashmir and Pakistan-administered Kashmir. Kashmir has been the target of a campaign of militancy by all sides in the conflict. Thousands of lives have been lost since 1989 due to the intensified insurgency 1989, a widespread armed insurgency started in Kashmir with the disputed 1987 election; since after 1987 rigged Sate elections some of the 'states legislative assembly' 'formed militant wings' later on after the disputed rigged election and furthermore that had started a catalyst for the insurgency , Casualties include civilians, Kashmiri and Indian Armed Forces and foreign militants.

The Inter-Services Intelligence of Pakistan has been accused by India of supporting and training Mujahideen to fight in Jammu and Kashmir. While, International Human Right Groups have accused Indian army of committing grave Human rights violations in Indian-administered Jammu and Kashmir.

According to official figures released in Jammu and Kashmir assembly (Indian controlled), there were 3,400 disappearance cases and the insurgency has left more than 47,000 people dead till July 2009. However, the number of insurgency-related deaths in the state have fallen sharply since the start of a slow-moving peace process between India and Pakistan.

Militancy and Military

Though there had been instances of sporadic conflict in many regions for many years, intensified attacks occurred in the late 1980s, when the 1987 state elections were rigged although disputed; had resulted in some of the 'states legislative assembly' 'formed militant wings' later on after the election forming and creating the catalyst for the insurgency. However Indian Government believes Mujahideen fighters from Afghanistan slowly infiltrated the region, with Pakistan's help, following the end of the Soviet-Afghan War in 1989. Since then, violence has increased significantly in strength. Many separatists have carried out attacks on local Hindus, Indian civilians and Indian army installations in response to what they see as Indian army occupation.

India frequently asserts that most of the separatist militant groups are based in Pakistan and Pakistan-administered Kashmir (also known as Azad Kashmir). Some like the All Parties Hurriyat Conference and the Jammu and Kashmir Liberation Front, demand an independent Kashmir. Other militant groups such as Lashkar-e-Toiba and Jaish-e-Mohammed favour a Pakistani-Kashmir. These groups have contacts with Taliban and Bin Laden. Both the organizations no longer operate under these names after they were banned by the Indian and Pakistani government and by other countries including the US and UK. Of the larger militant groups, the Hizbul Mujahideen, a militant organization based in Indian administered Kashmir, unlike other groups, has only kept its name. Despite casualties, the militants are still believed to number thousands rather than hundreds. Several new separatist organizations have also emerged. According to US Intelligence, Al-Qaeda also has a main base in Pakistani Kashmir and is helping to foment terrorism in Jammu and Kashmir. However India, Pakistan and the separatist organizations call this as hoax. Inspector General Police, Kashmir range also referred this as a hoax.

It is hard to determine the total number of casualties. According to a report by the Government of India in the year 2000, 31,000 Indian civilians had lost their lives due to the insurgency. Human rights groups and local NGOs put the total figure at more than 84,000 (2005 figure). Militancy had reached its peak in 1994 when the region saw more than 6,043 incidents and has since declined. However, Kashmir continues to remain as the most volatile region in the world with an average of 2,500 incidents every year. According to an Indian estimate in 2005 there were about 2,000 militants in the Kashmir valley alone; 1,200 of them belong to the Hizbul Mujahideen. Not all Kashmiri separatists and militant organizations share the same ideology. Some fight in the name of religion, some are openly pro-Pakistan and some favour an independent Kashmir.

Due to the presence of these numerous anti-India insurgent groups India has been compelled to deploy massive number of troops in the Indian administered *Jammu and Kashmir* for the task of counter insurgency. New Delhi has never made an official count, but military analysts estimate that anywhere from 30,000 to nearly 33,000 security personnel are most likely involved, supported by thousands of Indian paramilitary groups such as the Rashtriya Rifles and the Romeo Force (all a part of Indian Army).

In a 'Letter to American People' written by Osama bin Laden in 2002 he stated that one of the reasons he was fighting America is because of her support to India on the Kashmir issue. In 2002 U.S. Secretary of Defense Donald Rumsfeld on a trip to Delhi suggested that Al-Qaeda was active in Kashmir. An investigation in 2002 unearthed evidence that Al-Qaeda and its affiliates were prospering in Pakistan-administered Kashmir with tacit approval of Pakistan's National Intelligence agency Inter-Services Intelligence Also US Intelligence agencies believe that Al-Qaeda and Taliban are helping organize a terror campaign in Kashmir to foment conflict between India and Pakistan. A 2001 report 'Pakistan's Role in the Kashmir Insurgency' of US Think Tank RAND Corporation noted that 'More intrinsically, the nature of the Kashmir conflict has been transformed from what was originally a secular, locally- based struggle (conducted via the Jammu Kashmir Liberation Front — JKLF) to one that is now largely carried out by foreign militants and rationalized in pan-Islamic religious terms.' In July 2006 Al-Qaeda stated that it had established a wing in Kashmir.

Militant Groups

Over the last two years, a militant group, Lashkar-e-Toiba has split into two factions: *Al Mansurin* and *Al Nasirin*. Another new group reported to have emerged is the Save Kashmir Movement. Harkat-ul-Mujahideen (formerly known as Harkat-ul-Ansar) and Lashkar-e-Toiba are believed to be operating from Muzaffarabad, Azad Kashmir and Muridke, Pakistan respectively. Other less well known groups are the Freedom Force and Farzandan-e-Milat. A smaller group, Al-Badr, has been active in Kashmir for many years and is still believed to be functioning. All Parties Hurriyat Conference, an organisation that uses moderate means to press for the rights of the Kashmiris, is often considered as the *mediator* between New Delhi and insurgent groups.

Not much is known about collaboration between the various groups, but most say they are members of an alliance known as the United Jihad Council (UJC). The two groups which India says were behind the December 2001 attack on the Indian Parliament in New Delhi – known then as Jaish-e-Mohammed and Lashkar-e-Toiba are believed to be members of the *UJC*. India says that it was Jaish-e-Mohammed that attacked the Jammu and Kashmir State Assembly in Srinagar in October 2001. It is also known that the Jaish-e-Mohammed was responsible for the hijacking of Indian Airlines Flight

IC-814 to Kandahar, which forced the Government of India to release Maulana Masood Azhar, the chief of the Jaish-e-Mohammed. Recruits from various parts of the world have been sent to Pakistan-administered Kashmir for training and advice.

India and Pakistan

A 1994 report by Human Rights Watch group lends support to both Indian and Pakistani charges. In support of Indian claims, it states that "

There is compelling evidence that elements of the Pakistani government have sponsored a significant flow of arms to Kashmiri militants [from arms bazaars in the North-West Frontier Province], as well as an extensive training programme.

While in support of Pakistani claims, its states that "*the human rights record of the Indian government in Punjab and Kashmir is appalling. Abuses in Kashmir are clearly on the rise.*" The US government has also supported the claim that anti-India terror groups exist in India. India claims that there are also other Afghan, Egyptian, Yemeni and Bangladeshi terrorists active in Jammu and Kashmir. The Council on Foreign Relations states that Pakistan's military and Inter-Services Intelligence (ISI) both include personnel who sympathize with—or even assist—Islamist militants adding that "ISI has provided covert but well-documented support to terrorist groups active in Kashmir, among other outfits." In a recent infiltration bid, a Pakistan Army officer was shot dead, with India citing that this was clear and conclusive evidence of Pakistani involvement in the insurgency.

The UN Security Council has also confirmed the existence of terrorist groups based in [Pakistani] Kashmir and urged Pakistan to crack down on terrorist groups which had been operating in Kashmir and killing innocent people.

Pakistan describes the separatists as "freedom fighters" and says that it supports their effort for the cause of the Kashmiris only morally and diplomatically. Pakistan however admits that there has been 'cross border infiltration of militants' across the Line of Control. In 2008, Pakistani President Asif Ali Zardari said India has never been a threat to Pakistan and that militants in Kashmir are terrorists. In 2002, Pakistani President Pervez Musharraf tried to clamp down on the militants operating from Pakistan. India, however, claims that Islamabad supports these groups financially and militarily. Sources have maintained that Pakistan's intelligence organisation, Inter Services Intelligence, is the main supplier of funds and arms to these groups; a claim that Islamabad has dismissed. According to the Indian news site Rediff.com, British Government had stated in 2002 that there is a 'clear link' between Pakistan's Inter Services Intelligence and three major militant groups *An article* in *The Guardian* had uncovered evidence that Pakistani militants were openly raising funds and training new recruits and that the ISI's Kashmir Cell was instrumental in funding and controlling the militant outfits. Richard Bennett, a British military and intelligence analyst states that the ISI has armed and trained generations of Islamist extremists and has directed many of their attacks both within the Kashmir and in India's major cities.

Indian sources also allege that there are between 2,600 to 3,000 militants receiving training in camps across Pakistan and Pakistan Administered Kashmir. During a peace summit between former Pakistani President Pervez Musharraf and Indian former-Prime Minister Atal Bihari Vajpayee in January 2004, Islamabad assured India that it would do everything possible to curb the activities any training camps on its territory. However, violence has continued in Kashmir despite a 3 year long peace process between India and Pakistan. There were as many as 166 incidents in June 2005 alone in which some 201 people have died.

According to Indian sources there are about 37 training camps in Pakistan, 49 in Azad Kashmir and 22 in Afghanistan. The FBI also has produced images of camps operating in Pakistan. India claims that every year thousands of armed insurgents infiltrate into Indian-administered Kashmir and carry out attacks against Indian Security Forces and Kashmiri civilians. In June 2005, the Indian Army had foiled at least 72 infiltration attempts along the Line of Control in Kashmir. India alleges that despite the commitments made by Pervez Musharraf, Islamabad has done little to stop the training camps on its soil. According to India, most of the militants in Kashmir come from Pakistan, Afghanistan, Egypt, Yemen and Bangladesh. Not all Kashmiri separatists and militant organizations share the same ideology. Some fight in the name of religion, some are pro-Pakistan and some favour an independent Kashmir. While the vast majority of militants are Muslims, one report indicated a minority of fighter (40 to 50) are Hindu militants who have either taken up arms or provided safe cover for militants.

Human Rights Violations

Human Rights Violations by Militants

Militants are accused of violence against the Kashmir populace. Thousands of civilian Kashmiris (Hindus, Sikhs, Buddhists and Muslims have been killed in Kashmir over the past 10 years by militants organizations. Human rights organizations put the figure of the number of civilians killed between 1 January 1999 and 31 December 1999 at about 9,733.. According to official figures released in 2009, Indian Health and Family Welfare Minister Ghulam Nabi Azad, a Kashmiri himself and former Chief Minister of Jammu and Kashmir said 14,808 Muslims lost their lives while 1,748 Hindus and 115 Sikhs were killed during the rein of militancy in the state since 1989 by militants.

Tens of thousands of Kashmiri Pandits have emigrated as a result of the violence. Estimates of the displaced varies from 170,000 to 700,000. Thousands of Pandits have to move to Jammu because of terrorism. On 15 February 2006 United States Congressman Frank Pallone introduced a resolution in United States House of Representatives condemning the violation of Human rights of Kashmiri Pandits. He stated that an ethnic cleansing campaign was being run by Islamic terrorists to convert Kashmir into a Muslim state and 400,000 Kashmiri Pandits had either been murdered or displaced from their homes. The resolution was passed by the House (with Senate concurring) and stated that (1) Congress condemns the human rights violations committed against Kashmiri Pandits in the strongest terms (2) it is the sense of Congress that the Government of the Republic of India and the State Government of Jammu and Kashmir should take immediate steps to remedy the situation of the Kashmiri Pandits and should act to ensure the physical, political and economic security of this embattled community and (3) Congress supports mutual discussions between the Government of India and the State Government of Jammu and Kashmir to achieve a peaceful and equitable solution to the Kashmiri conflict that is acceptable to the Kashmiri Pandits while ensuring that they are a part of the ongoing dialogue.

Human Rights Violations by Pakistan

Human rights violations have also been reported in Pakistan-administered Kashmir. A 2-day conference on Gilgit Baltistan was held on April 8–9, 2008 at the European Parliament in Brussels under the auspices of International Kashmir Alliance. Here several members of the European Parliament (MEPs) expressed concern over the human rights violation in Gilgit Baltistan and urged the government of Pakistan to establish democratic institutions and rule of law in this area of northern Kashmir. Abdul Hamid Khan,

Chairman Balawaristan National Front speaking at the same conference said "no democratically elected representative (from Gilgit Baltistan) was included when Karachi Agreement was signed between Pakistan and Muslim Conference leaders in 1949." On 25 April 2007 European Union published a report entitled 'on Kashmir: present situation and future prospects'. Section 2 of the noted the absence of democracy in Gilgit Baltistan region and in section 32 deplored the human rights violations in this region. A 2008 report by the United Nations High Commissioner for Refugees determined that Pakistan administered Kashmir, was 'Not Free'. It also criticized the Pakistani Government saying 'The appropriation of land in the Northern Areas by non-Kashmiri migrants from elsewhere in Pakistan, with the tacit encouragement of the federal government and army, has led to dwindling economic opportunities for the local population and an increase in sectarian tension between the majority Shia Muslims and a growing number of Sunnis.' The same report determined that the Indian administered Jammu and Kashmir was 'Partly Free'. Parties like Balawaristan National Front are fighting for independence of Pakistan-administered Kashmir from Pakistan.

Human Rights Violations by India

A 1996 Human Rights Watch report accuses the Indian military and Indian-government backed paramilitaries of "committ serious and widespread human rights violations in Kashmir." One such alleged massacre occurred on 6 January 1993 in the town of Sopore. *TIME Magazine* described the incident as such: "In retaliation for the killing of one soldier, paramilitary forces rampaged through Sopore's market setting buildings ablaze and shooting bystanders. The Indian government pronounced the event 'unfortunate' and claimed that an ammunition dump had been hit by gunfire, setting off fires that killed most of the victims." In addition to this, there have been claims of disappearances by the police or the army in Kashmir by several human rights organizations.

Many human rights organizations such as Amnesty International and the Human Rights Watch (HRW) have condemned human rights abuses in Kashmir by Indians such as "extra-judicial executions", "disappearances" and torture; the "Armed Forces Special Powers Act", which "provides impunity for human rights abuses and fuels cycles of violence. The Armed Forces Special Powers Act (AFSPA) grants the military wide powers of arrest, the right to shoot to kill and to occupy or destroy property in counterinsurgency operations. Indian officials claim that troops need such powers because the army is only deployed when national security is at serious risk from armed combatants. Such circumstances, they say, call for extraordinary measures." Human rights organizations have also asked Indian government to repeal the Public Safety Act, since "a detainee may be held in administrative detention for a maximum of two years without a court order.".

A 2008 report by the United Nations High Commissioner for Refugees determined that Indian Administered Kashmir, was only 'partly Free' .

Militant Acts in J&K

- July and August 1989 - 3 CRPF personnel and politician Mohd. Yusuf Halwai of NC/F were killed.
- 1989 kidnapping of Rubaiya Sayeed daughter of the then Home Minister of India Mufti Sayeed.
- 1995 kidnapping of western tourists in Jammu and Kashmir 6 foreign trekkers from Anantnag district were kidnapped by Al Faran, One was beheaded later, one escaped and other four remain untraced presumable killed.

- 1997 Sangrampora massacre - On 21 March 1997, 7 Kashmiri Pandits were killed in Sangrampora village in the Budgam district.
- Wandhama Massacre - In January 1998, 24 Kashmiri Pandits living in the village of Wandhama were massacred by Pakistani militants. According to the testimony of one of the survivors, the militants dressed themselves as officers of the Indian Army, entered their houses and then started firing blindly. The incident was significant because it coincided with former US president Bill Clinton's visit to India and New Delhi used the massacre to present a case against the alleged Pakistan-supported terrorism in Kashmir.
- 1998 Prankote massacre - 26 Hindu villagers of Udhampur district were killed by militants.
- 1998 Champanari massacre - 25 Hindu villagers killed on 19 June 1998 by Islamic militants.
- 2001 terrorist attack on Jammu and Kashmir legislative assembly On 1 October 2001, a bombing at the Legislative Assembly in Srinagar killed 38.
- 2002 Qasim Nagar massacre - 29 Hindu labourers were killed in Jammu by militants on July 13, 2002.
- 2003 Nadimarg Massacre - 24 Hindus killed in Nadimarg, Kashmir on 23 March 2003 by Lashkar-e-Toiba militants.
- Qasim Nagar Attack - On 13 July 2003, armed militants believed to be a part of the Lashkar-e-Toiba threw hand grenades at the Qasim Nagar market in Srinagar and then fired on civilians standing nearby killing 27 and injuring many more.
- 20 July 2005 Srinagar Bombing - A car bomb exploded near an armoured Indian Army vehicle in the famous

Church Lane area in Srinagar killing 4 Indian Army personnel, one civilian and the suicide bomber. Militant group Hizbul Mujahideen, claimed responsibility for the attack.

- Budshah Chowk attack - A militant attack on 29 July 2005 at Srinigar's city centre, Budshah Chowk, killed 2 and left more than 17 people injured. Most of those injured were media journalists.
- Assassination of Ghulam Nabi Lone - On 18 October 2005 suspected Kashmiri militants killed Jammu and Kashmir's then education minister Ghulam Nabi Lone. Militant group called Al Mansurin claimed responsibility for the attack. Abdul Ghani Lone, a prominent All Party Hurriyat Conference leader, was assassinated by unidentified gunmen during a memorial rally in Srinagar. The assassination resulted in wide-scale demonstrations against the Indian forces for failing to provide enough security cover for Mr. Lone.
- On 3 May 2006 militants massacred 35 Hindus in Doda and Udhampur districts in Jammu and Kashmir.
- On 12 June 2006 one person was killed and 31 were wounded when terrorists hurled three grenades on Vaishnodevi shrine-bound buses at the general bus stand here this morning.
- 2 June 2009': 17-year-old Nigeen Awan was shot and killed at her residence by Militants.
- 16 June 2009: 45-year-old Rashma Jan died when terrorists barged into her house at Sopore on 16 June and fired indiscriminately.

Recent Developments

Violent activities in the region declined in 2004. There are two main reasons for this: warming of relations between

New Delhi and Pakistan which consequently lead to a ceasefire between the two countries in 2003 and the fencing of the LOC being carried out by the Indian Army. Moreover, coming under intense international pressure, Islamabad was compelled to take actions against the militants' training camps on its territory. In 2004, the two countries also agreed upon decreasing the number of troops present in the region.

Under pressure, Kashmiri militant organizations have made an offer for talks and negotiations with New Delhi, which was accepted by India. India's Border Security Force blamed the Pakistani military for providing cover-fire for the militants whenever they infiltrated into Indian territory from Pakistan. However, ever since the ceasefire has come into action, the militants have received no back-up from Pakistani Military, which has contributed significantly to the decline in *cross-border terrorism* in the state. Even the recently elected Pakistani President, Asif Ali Zardari admitted that the militants operating in Kashmir were indeed terrorists""

2008

According to Government of India Home Ministry, 2008 marks the lowest civilian casualties in 20 years with 89 deaths, compared to highest of 1,413 in 1996. 85 security personnel died in 2008 compared to 613 in 2001. Human right situation improved with only 1 custodial death and no custodial disappearance.

2009

- Hizbul Mujahideen founder, considered founder of terrorism in Kashmir, Ahsan Dar was arrested on 14 January.
- **Feberuary 21, 2009**: Bomai Killing: Army kills two devotees in an indiscriminate firing incident by 22nd Battalion of Rashtriya Rilfes in Bomai, Sopore. Which results in a massive valley wide protests.

- **6 March 2009**: Nowhatta Killing: A CRPF vehicle killed one youth and crushed another at Nawhatta during a protest. The killing triggered violent protests across the city. Authorities clamed curfew for continuously for four days.
- Separatists and workers of a political party were believed to be behind stone pelting incidents which generally leads to retaliatory fire by the police. Autorickshaw laden with stones meant for distribution was seized by the police in 11 March 2009.
- **18 March 2009**: Rajpora killing: Barely a few hours after the union home minister, P Chidambaram, assured action against troopers found guilty for Bomai killings, 181 bn of paramilitary CRPF troopers shot dead a carpenter, Ghulam Mohiudin Malik son of Muhammad Akbar Malik, at Khaigam Pakherpora in south Kashmir's Pulwama district.
- **31 May 2009**: **Shopian rape and murder case:**Protests over rape and murder of two young women allegedly by Indian Armed Forces. Pro-freedom leaders arrested and police and paramilitary forces resorted to firing at protesters in several places, including Shopian, Baramulla and Srinagar killing one person and injuring hundreds.
- **18 August 2009**: Government stated there had been 3429 youth missing since 1990 — till date. However local and international rights groups have suggested over 8,000 people have disappeared in the region.
- **9 September 2009**: An Indian army major and three militants were killed in an encounter in the Mendhar area of Poonch district in Jammu and Kashmir. Indian army had earlier pointed out that there has been an increase in the activity on the western border. Anti-

India militant outfits have been trying to push in as much men, money and weapons on to the Indian side before snow blocks their passage.

- **2 December 2009**: A Kashmir based group, International People's Tribunal on Human Rights and Justice, said that it had found 2600 bodies in unmarked graves during a three year survey. While the group did not who was the buried were, it alleged that some could be innocent people killed by security force and called for an investigation.
- **18 December 2009**: India withdraws 30,000 troops from Kashmir in one of the largest troop withdrawal' in response to dramatic improvement in security situation.

2010

- **6 January 2010**: A militant attack on a police station in Srinagar triggers a 20 hour gun battle between Lashkar-e-Taiba militants and Indian police. Two militants, one police officer and one civilian were reported killed.
- **29 January 2010**: Rebel attack kills 2 Indian soldiers in Kashmir.

8
Khalistan Movement and Sikh Extremism

The goal of the Khalistan movement is or was to create a Sikh homeland, often called *Khâlistân* ("The Land of the Pure"), in the Punjab region of India. Harking back to the 18th century Sikh Empire, the envisioned Sikh state would include all Punjabi-speaking areas in Greater Punjab.

The movement reached its zenith in 1970s and 1980s. Now-a-days, it is widely seen as a smaller scale movement. There are claims of funding from other nations to attract young people into militant groups, who are looking to get an independent Sikh homeland through donations from foreign Sikh supporters.

In 1971, Khalistan proponent Jagjit Singh Chauhan, travelled to the United States. He placed an advertisement in *The New York Times* proclaiming the formation of Khalistan and was able to collect millions of dollars.

On April 12, 1980, he held a meeting with Indira Gandhi before declaring the formation of "National Council of Khalistan", at Anandpur Sahib. He declared himself to be the President and Balbir Singh Sandhu as its Secretary General. In May 1980, Jagjit Singh Chauhan travelled to London and announced the formation of Khalistan. A similar announcement was made by Balbir Singh Sandhu, in Amritsar, who released stamps and currency of Khalistan. The inaction of the authorities in Amritsar and elsewhere was decried by Akali Dal headed by Longowal as a political stunt by the Congress (I) party.

In the 1980s, some Khalistan proponents turned to militancy, resulting in Indian Army's counter-militancy operations. In one such operation, Operation Blue Star, the Indian Army forcibly entered the Harmandir Sahib (often called the Golden Temple). The handling of the operation, damage to the Akal Takht (which is one of the five seats of temporal physical religious authority of the Sikhs) and loss of life on both sides, led to widespread criticism of the Indian Government. Many Sikhs strongly maintain that the attack resulted in the desecration of the holiest Sikh shrine. Indian Prime Minister Indira Gandhi was assassinated by her two Sikh bodyguards and many thousands of Sikhs were massacred in the following riots. In January 1986, the Golden Temple was occupied by militants belonging to All India Sikh Students Federation and Damdami Taksal. On January 26, 1986, the gathering passed a resolution (*gurmattâ*) favouring the creation of Khalistan. Khalistan was envisaged by its proponents as a Sikh-majority state, which opponents argued would become a theocracy.

Under the Constitution of India, secessionism is forbidden and various rebel groups in favour of Khalistan fought an insurgency against the Government of India. Indian security forces suppressed the major secessionist insurgency in Punjab in the early 1990s, but several Indian Sikh political parties are still fighting for independent Khalistan through peaceful means inside India and international pro-Khalistan organizations such as Dal Khalsa (International) are still active outside India.

Origins

Partition of India

India was partitioned on a religious basis in 1947 on its independence. Punjab was split between Pakistan and India.

Before independence the Sikhs were not in majority in any of the pre-partition Punjab districts. Among the three religions (Islam, Hinduism, Sikhism), the Sikhs formed the largest group (41.6%) only in the Ludhiana district. For the purpose of partition, the Hindus and the Sikhs were grouped together. The Sikhs were staunchly opposed to the concept of a separate Pakistan. The Sikh population that was as high as 19.8% in 1941 some districts that went to Pakistan, dropped to 0.1% in all of them and it rose sharply in the districts assigned to India.

With the possibility of an end to British colonialism in sight, the Sikh leadership appointed Gurjeet Johal from village Pandwa as their new leader. She became concerned about the future of the Sikhs. The Sikhs and the Muslims had unsuccessfully claimed separate representation for their communities in the Morley-Minto Reforms of 1909. With the Muslims proposing the creation of Pakistan, some Sikhs put forth the idea of likewise carving out a Sikh state, Khalistan. In the 1940s, a prolonged negotiation transpired between the British and the three Indian groups seeking political power, namely, the Hindus, the Muslims and the Sikhs. During this period Mohandas Karamchand Gandhi stated that the resolution was adopted by the Congress to satisfy the Sikh community.

Jawaharlal Nehru reiterated Gandhi's assurance to the Sikhs at the All India Congress Committee meeting in Calcutta in 1946. Nehru assured the Sikhs that they would be allowed to function as a semi-autonomous unit so that they may have a sense of freedom. This was formalized through a resolution passed by the Indian Constituent Assembly on 9, December, 1946.

Controversies

During a press conference on 10, July, 1946 in Bombay, Nehru made a controversial statement to the effect that the

Congress may "change or modify" the federal arrangement agreed upon for independent India for the betterment towards a united India; this claim outraged many. Some Sikhs felt that they had been "tricked" into joining the Indian union. On 21 November, 1949, during the review of the draft of the Indian Constitution, Hukam Singh, a Sikh representative, declared to the Constituent Assembly:

> "Naturally, under these circumstances, as I have stated, the Sikhs feel utterly disappointed and frustrated. They feel that they have been discriminated against. Let it not be misunderstood that the Sikh community has agreed to this [Indian] Constitution. I wish to record an emphatic protest here. My community cannot subscribe its assent to this historic document."

Allegations of Discrimination against Sikhs (1947-1966)

Punjab in India was a Hindu majority state (63.7%) until 1966, when it was partitioned to remove the Hindu majority districts, as a result of demands made by Sikh leaders for a Punjabi Suba. The state now has a slight (59.9% in 2001) Sikh majority.

Kapur Singh, a Deputy Commissioner (senior government official in the Indian bureaucracy) and a member of the Indian Civil Service, had been dismissed from service on charges of corruption. After he was dismissed, he published a pamphlet, in which he alleged that Prime Minister Nehru, through Governor Chandu Lal Trivedi, had issued a directive in 1947 to all the Commissioners in Punjab to the effect that the Sikhs in general must be treated as a criminal tribe.

> "In 1947, the governor of Punjab, Mr. C.M. Trevedi, in deference to the wishes of the Prime Minister Jawaharlal Nehru and Sardar Patel, the Deputy Prime Minister, issued certain instructions to all the Deputy Commissioners of Indian Punjab...These were to the effect that, without reference to the law of the land, the Sikhs in general and Sikh migrants in particular must be treated as a "criminal tribe". Harsh treatment must

> be meted out to them...to the extent of shooting them dead so that they wake up to the political realities and recognise "who are the rulers and who the subjects"."

Pritam Singh Gill, a retired Principal of Lyallpur Khalsa College, Jalandhar, also made allegations of "the Hindu conspiracy to destroy Sikhs; kill the language, kill the culture, kill the community."

Sikh writer Khushwant Singh writes, however, that there was no truth whatsoever in Nehru ever having sent out such a directive, nor was Kapur Singh a victim of any conspiracy against him. This pamphlet is thus largely regarded as a hoax. Nevertheless, Kapur Singh won the favour of Akali leader Tara Singh who assisted him in winning the election into the Punjab Legislature and then to the Lok Sabha.

Language Issues

In the 1950s and 1960s, linguistic issues in India caused civil disorder when the central government declared Hindi as the national language of India. The nationwide movement of linguistic groups seeking statehood resulted in a massive reorganisation of states according to linguistic boundaries in 1956. At that time, Indian Punjab had its capital in Shimla and though the vast majority of the Sikhs lived in Punjab, they still did not form a majority. But if Haryana and Himachal could be separated they could have a Punjab in which they could form a majority of 60 per cent against the Hindus being 40 per cent. The Akali Dal, a Sikh dominated political party active mainly in Punjab, sought to create a Punjabi Suba, or a Punjabi-speaking state. This case was presented to the States Reorganization Commission established in 1953. It is generally believed that the Hindus sensed what the Sikhs had in mind. They, supported by the Hindu newspapers from Jalandhar, exhorted Punjabi Hindus to declare Hindi as their "mother tongue" instead of Punjabi in the censuses that took place, so that the Sikhs could be deprived of the argument that they were only asking for a Punjabi-speaking Suba. The demand for adoption of Punjabi for Punjabi-speaking areas first created and later intensified the rift between Hindus and Sikhs of Punjab.

The States Reorganization Commission, not recognizing Punjabi as a language that was distinct grammatically from Hindi, rejected the demand for a Punjabi Suba or State. Another reason that the Commission gave in its report was that the movement lacked general support of the people inhabiting the region. Many Sikhs felt discriminated against by the commission.

River Waters Dispute

Before the creation of the Punjabi Suba, Punjab was the master of its river waters (The North Indian rivers – Sutlej, Beas, Ravi did not flow through any other state for any length). The trifurcation of the state led to three competing demands for these river waters and the central government decided to step in. The Central Government—against the provisions of the Indian Constitution—introduced sections 78 to 80 in the Punjab Reorganization Act, 1966, under which the central government "assumed the powers of control, maintenance, distribution and development of the waters and the hydel power of the Punjab rivers.". Many Sikhs perceived this division as unfair and as an anti Sikh measure, since the vast majority of the people of Punjab are dependent on agriculture.

Akali Dal's Demands

The Akali Dal led a series of peaceful mass demonstrations to present its grievances to the Central Government. The demands of the Akali Dal were based on the Anandpur Sahib Resolution, which was adopted by the party in October 1973 to raise specific political, economic and social issues. The major motivation behind the resolution was the safeguarding of the Sikh identity by securing a state structure that was decentralized, with non-interference from the Central Government. The Resolution outlines seven objectives.

1. The transfer of the federally administered city of Chandigarh to Punjab.
2. The transfer of Punjabi speaking and contiguous areas to Punjab.
3. Decentralization of states under the existing constitution, limiting the central government's role.
4. The call for land reforms and industrialisation of Punjab, along with safeguarding the rights of the weaker sections of the population.
5. The enactment of An all-India Gurdwara (Sikh House of Worship) Act.
6. Protection for minorities residing outside Punjab, but within India.
7. Revision of government's recruitment quota restricting the number of Sikhs in armed forces.

The Wall Street Journal noted:

"The Akali Dal is in the hands of moderate and sensible leadership...but giving anyone a fair share of power is unthinkable politics of Mrs. Gandhi [the then Prime Minister of India]...Many Hindus in Punjab privately concede that there isn't much wrong with these demands. But every time the ball goes to the Congress court, it is kicked out one way or another because Mrs. Gandhi considers it a good electoral calculation."

The Assassination of Lala Jagat Narain

In a politically charged environment, Lala Jagat Narain, the owner of the Hind Samachar group of newspapers and member of Indian National Congress, was assassinated by Sikh militants in September 1981. In September 1981, Bhindranwale was arrested for his alleged role in the assassination but was later released by the Punjab State Government, as no evidence was found against him.

The Khalistani movement can be considered to have effectively started from this point. Though there were a number of leaders vying for leadership role, most were based in United Kingdom and Canada and had limited influence. In Punjab, Bhindranwale was the unchallenged leader of the movement and made his residence in the Golden Temple in Amritsar. By convention, the Indian Army and the Punjab Police would not enter this religious building.

Dharam Yudh Morcha

In August 1982, the Akali Dal under the leadership of Harcharan Singh Longowal launched the Dharam Yudh Morcha, or the "battle for righteousness." Bhindranwale and the Akali Dal united; their goal was the fulfilment of demands based upon the Anandpur Sahib Resolution. In two and a half months, security forces arrested over thirty thousand Sikhs.

In November 1982, Akali Dal announced the organization of protests in Delhi during the Asian Games. The police were instructed to stop all buses, trains and vehicles that were headed for Delhi and interrogate Sikh passengers. The Sikhs as a community felt discriminated against by the Indian state. Later, the Akali Dal organized a convention at the Darbar Sahib attended by over 5,000 Sikh ex-servicemen, 170 of whom were above the rank of colonel. These Sikhs claimed that there was discrimination against them in government service.

Religious Confusion

During this turmoil, the Akali Dal began another agitation in February 1984 protesting against clause (2)(b) of Article 25 of the Indian Constitution, which ambiguously states "the reference to Hindus shall be construed as including a reference to persons professing the Sikh, Jain or Buddhist religion", though it also implicitly recognizes Sikhism as a separate religion with the words "the wearing and carrying of kirpans shall be deemed to be included in the profession of the Sikh religion.".

The Akali Dal members demanded that the constitution should remove any ambiguous statements that uses the word Hindu to refer to the Sikhs. For instance, a Sikh couple who marry in accordance to the rites of the Sikh religion must register their marriage either under the Special Marriages Act (1954) or the Hindu Marriage Act – the Akalis demanded replacement of such rules with Sikhism-specific laws. However, their demands were not taken seriously and several Akali leaders were arrested for burning the Indian constitution in protest. Thus, the Indian Government's implicit defining of its Sikh citizens as being part of the Hindu community created discontent among Sikhs, who feared a loss of identity.

OPERATION BLUESTAR

Operation *Blue Star* 3– 6 June 1984 was an Indian military operation ordered by Indira Gandhi, then Prime Minister of India, to remove Sikh separatists from the Golden Temple in Amritsar. The separatists, led by Jarnail Singh Bhindranwale, were amassing weapons in that gurudwara.

The operation was carried out by Indian army troops with tanks and armoured vehicles. Militarily successful, the operation aroused immense controversy and the government's justification for the timing and style of the attack are highly debated. Operation Blue Star was included in the Top 10 Political Disgraces by *India Today* magazine.

Official reports put the number of deaths among the Indian army at 83 and the number of civilian deaths at 492, though independent estimates ran much higher.

The impact of the military assault, its aftermath and the increased tensions led to assaults on members of the Sikh community within India and uproar amongst Sikhs worldwide "The assault, which the Sikhs themselves call the Ghallughara..." or massacre. In India, many Sikhs resigned from armed and civil administrative office and returned their government awards. Some who perceived the attack as desecration of the Sikh shrine pledged revenge. Indira Gandhi was assassinated by two of her Sikh bodyguards on 31, October, 1984 in her garden when she was going for an interview.

The Operation

Indira Gandhi first asked Lt. Gen. S.K. Sinha, then Vice-chief of Indian Army and who was to succeed as the Army Chief, to prepare a position paper for assault on the Golden Temple. Lt. Gen. Sinha advised against any such move, given its sacrilegious nature according to Sikh tradition. He suggested the government adopt an alternative solution. A controversial decision was made to replace him with General Arun Shridhar Vaidya as the Chief of the Indian Army. General Vaidya, assisted by Lt. Gen. K Sundarji as Vice-chief, planned and coordinated Operation Blue Star.

On 3 June, a 36-hour curfew was imposed on the state of Punjab with all methods of communication and public travel suspended. Electricity supplies were also interrupted, creating a total blackout and cutting off the state from the rest of India and the world. Complete censorship was enforced on the news media.

The Indian Army stormed the Golden Temple on the night of 5 June under the command of Kuldip Singh Brar.

The forces had full control of the Golden Temple by the morning of 7 June. There were casualties among the army, civilians and militants. Militant leaders Bhindranwale and Shabeg Singh were killed in the operation.

Operation Blue Star coincided with a Sikh annual festival. Pilgrims, including the elderly and children, were trapped inside the temple when the operation began and many were wounded and killed as a result.

Jarnail Singh Bhindranwale in the Golden Temple

Throughout his career Jarnail Singh Bhindranwale remained in contact with Indira Gandhi. Bhindranwale had earlier "taken refuge in" or "taken over" the Golden Temple and made it his headquarters in April 1980, when he was named as a suspect in the killing of Nirankari Baba Gurbachan Singh. The Nirankari Baba, also known as Baba Gurbachan Singh, had been the target of an attack by followers of a Sikh group, Akhand Kirtani Jatha, outside the Golden Temple when he appeared claiming himself to be the incarnation of Guru Gobind Singh. The Nirankaris are considered a heretical sect by the Khalsa. On 13 April 1978, Nirankari's Head Gurbachan Singh is alleged to have ridiculed 10th Guru Gobind Singh in a Nirankari Convention held in Amritsar and disrespected the Guru Granth Sahib. This prompted Akhand Kirtani Jatha to protest against the actions by Gurbachan Singh; his bodyguards responded by opening fire on the 13 Sikhs. The bodyguards of the Baba used guns to fire at the peaceful protesters. In the ensuing violence, several people were killed: two of Bhindranwale's followers, eleven Sikhs of the Akhand Kirtani Jatha and three Nirankaris. That event was allegedly premeditated by the Indian government with the Nirankaris subsequently acquitted of any wrong-doing by the courts, on grounds of self-defence.

In 1982, Bhindranwale and approximately 200 armed followers moved into a guest-house called the Guru Nanak

Niwas, in the precinct of the Golden Temple. From here he met and was interviewed by international television crews.

On 23, April, 1983, the Punjab Police Deputy Inspector General A. S. Atwal was shot dead as he left the Golden Temple compound. The following day, after the murder, Harchand Singh Longowal (then President of Shiromani Akali Dal) hinted at the involvement of the Chief Minister of the Punjab, Darbara Singh, in the murder.

On 15, December, 1983, Bhindranwale was forced to move out of Guru Nanak Niwas house by members of the Babbar Khalsa who acted with Harcharan Singh Longowal's support Longowal by now feared for his own safety. By 1983, the Golden Temple became a shelter for a large number of militants.

The Golden Temple compound and some of the surrounding houses were fortified. The Statesman reported on 4 July that light machine-guns and semi-automatic rifles were known to have been brought into the compound. On 1, February, 1984, Harcharan Singh Longowal claimed that Bhindranwale had suggested to him that motorcycles and arms should be purchased on a mass scale for killing members of a "particular community". Bhindranwale angrily responded to the allegation, saying "nothing is more farther in my mind than this".

Faced with imminent army action and with the foremost Sikh political organization, Shiromani Akali Dal (headed by Harchand Singh Longowal), abandoning him, Bhindranwale declared "This bird is alone. There are many hunters after it".

Time magazine reported (about Amritsar) that:

"These days it more closely resembles a city of death. Inside the temple compound, fierce Sikh warriors wield submachine guns, guarding against encroachment by government security forces. Outside, the security men keep a nervous vigil, all too aware that the bodies of murdered comrades often turn up in the warren of tiny streets around the shrine."

Overview

Operation Blue Star was launched to eliminate the Sikh militants who had sought cover in the Amritsar Golden Temple Complex. The Sikh militants within the Harminder Sahib were led by Jarnail Singh Bhindranwale and former Maj. Gen. Shabeg Singh. Maj. Gen. Kuldip Singh Brar had command of the action, operating under Gen. Sunderji.

20:00 hrs–22:00 hrs

The first element was the destruction of Shabeg Singh's outer defences. Much of this had been completed in the preliminary shelling. Major-General Brar had hoped to force Jarnail Singh Bhindranwale into surrendering, which did not occur. The destroyed defences included seventeen houses which the police believed Bhindranwale's followers occupied in the alleys surrounding the Golden Temple. Nearby was the Brahmbuta Akhara, a large building housing the headquarters of a Sikh sect. Then there were three main towers which had been fortified to create positions from which Bhindranwale's men could defend. Because the towers rose well above surrounding buildings, they were excellent observation positions for tracking the movement of Indian troops in the narrow alleys surrounding the temple. The tops of these towers were destroyed in the preliminary artillery fire.

22:00 hrs–23:30 hrs

Between 10:00 and 10:30 on 5 June commandos from 1st Battalion, the Parachute Regiment, were ordered to run down the steps under the clock tower on to the parikarma, ("pavement") and move quickly around the edge of the sacred pool to the Akal Takht. As the paratroopers entered the main gateway to the Temple they were gunned down by light machine-gun fire from both sides of the steps. The few commandos who did get down the steps were driven back by a barrage of fire from the building on the south side of the sacred pool. In the control room, a house on the opposite side of the clock-tower, Major-General Brar was waiting with two supporting officers to hear confirmation that the commandos had established positions inside the complex.

The few commandos left regrouped in the square outside and reported back to Maj. Gen. Brar. He ordered them to make another attempt. The commandos were then to be followed by the 10th Battalion of the Guards, commanded by Lieutenant-Colonel Israr Khan. This second commando attack managed to neutralize the machine-gun posts on both sides of the steps and get down on to the parikarma. They were followed by the Guards who came under heavy fire and were not able to make any progress. They radioed for permission to fire back at the buildings on the other side of the tank. That would have meant that the Golden Temple itself, which is in the middle of the pool, would have been in the line of fire. Brar initially refused, but started to receive reports of heavy casualties from the commander of the Guards.

23:30 hrs –01:00 hrs

Brar again requested tanks after an APC was destroyed by a rocket fired by a Sikh militant. His request was granted and seven tanks rolled into the Golden Temple complex. They cleared the ramparts and later assaulted the main temple in order to neutralize the militants remaining in the structure. The shelling achieved its objective and the primary target of removing militants from the Akal Takht was achieved by 01:00. However, the secondary objective of removing militants from other neighbouring structures went on for a further 24 hours.

Casualties

The Indian Army suffered 83 deaths, which included four officers, four Junior Commissioned Officers and 75 other ranks. 13 Indian Army Officers, 16 JCOs and 220 other ranks were injured in the operation. Indian Army recorded 492 civilian deaths inside Golden Temple with 433 persons segregated as "separatists" amongst 1592 persons apprehended. During June 1984, Rao served as Commander of 350 Infantry Brigade based in Jalandhar, which formed part of Ninth Infantry Division of Indian Army.

The Army placed total casualties at:

- Military: 83 killed, 248 wounded
- Militant Casualties: 492 killed, 86 wounded.

Independent historians placed the figure at:

- Military: 500
- Militant Casualties: 50.

According to some journalists, several Sikh youths were also killed in crossfire from militants. Unofficial casualty figures were much higher.

Aftermath

An unspecified number of Sikh soldiers resigned from positions across India in protest, with some reports of large-scale pitched battles being fought to bring mutineers under control.

The operation also led to the assassination of Prime Minister Indira Gandhi on 31, October, 1984 by two of her Sikh bodyguards, triggering the 1984 anti-Sikh riots. The widespread killing of Sikhs, principally in the national capital Delhi but also in other major cities in North India, led to major divisions between the Sikh community and the Indian Government. The Army withdrew from the Golden Temple later in 1984 under pressure from Sikh demands.

General A.S. Vaidya, the Chief of Army Staff at the time of Operation Blue Star, was assassinated in 1986 in Pune by two Sikhs, Harjinder Singh Jinda and Sukhdev Singh Sukha. Both were sentenced to death and hanged on 7 October, 1992.

Sikh militants continued to use and occupy the temple compound and on 1, May, 1986, Indian paramilitary police entered the temple and arrested 200 militants that had occupied the Golden Temple for more than three months. On 2, May, 1986 the paramilitary police undertook a 12-hour operation to take control of the Golden Temple at Amritsar from several hundred militants, but almost all the major radical leaders managed to escape.

In May 1988, Army troops were called in again to remove militants from the temple. The conflict of 12–18 May resulted in the clearance of the compound and regular worship resumed on 23 May. On 29 May, the government banned both political and military use of shrines in India.

In June 1990, the Indian Government ordered the area surrounding the temple to be vacated by local residents in order to prevent militant activity around the temple.

Criticisms

The use of artillery in the congested inner city of Amritsar proved deadly to many civilian bystanders living near the Golden Temple. The media blackout throughout the Punjab resulted in widespread doubt regarding the official stories and aided the promotion of hearsay and rumour. The operation is criticised on four main grounds, the choice of time of attack by Government, heavy casualty, loss of property and allegation of human rights violations by Army personnel.

"Last Resort"

The attack on Golden Temple was in plans even before the armed Sikh militants fortified it. Then GOC of the Indian Army, S.K. Sinha who was sacked at the last moment had criticised the Government's claim that the attack represented a "last resort", stating that the attack was planned a year and a half prior to the actual day of attack. S.K. Sinha and Mark Tully report that the Army had been rehearsing the attack in a replica of the Golden Temple at a secret location near Chakrata Cantonment in the Doon Valley.

Timing

The timing of Operation Blue Star coincided with a Sikh religious day, the martyrdom of Guru Arjan Dev, the founder of the Golden Temple. Sikhs from all over the world visit the temple on this day. In 1736 the Golden Temple was attacked by the Mughal Army, resulting in heavy casualties of civilian Sikhs. The attack of Ahmad Shah Abdali on the Golden Temple (Darbar Sahib) also came on Vaisakhi day when Sikhs gather in large numbers in Amritsar. Many Sikhs view the timing and attack by the Indian Army as an attempt to inflict maximum casualties on Sikhs and demoralize them and the government is in turn blamed for the inflated number of civilian dead for choosing to attack on this day.

The Sikh community's anger and suffering was further increased by comments from leading newspaper editors, such as Ramnath Goenka, terming the operation as "A greater victory than the win over Bangladesh, this is the greatest victory of Mrs. Gandhi".

During the operation the Sikh Reference Library caught fire and many rare books and manuscripts were destroyed. There are allegations that the Army also confiscated many books which were never returned, but the Army denies this.

Media Blackout

Before the attack by Army a media blackout was imposed in Punjab. The Times reporter Michael Hamlyn reported that journalists were picked up from their hotels at 5 a.m. in a military bus, taken to the adjoining border of the state of Haryana and "were abandoned there". The main towns in Punjab were put under curfew, transportation was banned, news blackout was imposed and Punjab was *"cut off from the outside world"*. A group of journalists who later tried to drive into Punjab were stopped at the road block at Punjab border and were threatened to be shot if they proceeded. The Indian nationals who worked with the foreign media were also banned. The press criticized these actions by Government as an "obvious attempt to attack the temple without the eyes of foreign press on them". Associated Press reporter Brahma Chellaney, who managed to report on the operation, later faced police intimidation.

Human Rights

Brahma Chellaney, who was then the South Asia correspondent of the Associated Press, was the only foreign reporter who managed to stay on in Amritsar despite the media blackout. His dispatches, filed by telex, provided the first non-governmental news reports on the bloody operation in Amritsar. His first dispatch, front-paged by the *New York Times, The Times of London and The Guardian,* reported a death toll about twice of what authorities had admitted. According to the dispatch, about 780 militants and civilians and 400 troops had perished in fierce gunbattles. The high casualty rates among security forces were attributed to "the presence of such sophisticated weapons as medium machine guns and rockets in the terrorists' arsenal." Mr. Chellaney also reported that "several" suspected Sikh militants had been shot with their hands tied. The dispatch, after its first paragraph reference to "several" such deaths, specified later that "eight to ten" men had been shot in that fashion. In that dispatch, Mr. Chellaney interviewed a doctor who said he was picked up by the Army and forced to conduct postmortems despite the fact he had never done any postmortem examination before. The number of casualties reported by Mr. Chellaney were far more than government reports and the Indian Government, which disputed his casualty figures accused him of inflammatory reporting. The Associated Press stood by the reports and figures, the accuracy of which was also "supported by Indian and other press accounts" according to Associated Press and reports in *The Times* and *The New York Times*.

C.K.C. Reddy, an Indian journalist writes that the

> "Whole of Punjab and especially the Golden Temple Complex was turned into a murderous mouse trap from where people could neither escape nor could they seek succour of any kind. The way the dead bodies were disposed off adds to the suspicions regarding the number and nature of the casualties. The bodies of the victims of military operation in Punjab were unceremoniously destroyed without any attempt to identify them and hand them over to their relatives. The government, after the operation, on the other hand, did every thing in its power to cover up the excesses of the army action. The most disturbing thing about the entire operation was that a whole mass of men, women and children were ordered to be killed merely on the suspicion that some terrorists were operating from the Golden Temple and other Gurdwaras."

Similar accusations of high handedness on part of Indian Army and allegations of human rights violation by security forces in Operation Blue Star and subsequent military operations in Punjab has been levelled by Justice V.M. Tarkunde, Mary Anne Weaver, human rights lawyer Ram Narayan Kumar and anthropologists Dr. Cynthia Mahmood. and Joyce Pettigrew.

The Indian Army responded to such criticism by simply stating that they "answered the call of duty as disciplined, loyal and dedicated members of the Armed Forces of India....our loyalties are to the nation, the armed forces to which we belong, the uniforms we wear and to the troops we command".

It was later pointed out that the blockade approach taken by Rajiv Gandhi five years later, in Operation Black Thunder when Sikh militants had again taken over the temple complex, was highly successful as they managed to resolve the stand-off peacefully and in hindsight Operation Blue Star could have been averted by using similar blockade tactics. The army responded by stating that "no comparison is possible between the two situations, as "there was no cult figure like Sant Bhindranwale to idolize and professional military general like Shahbeg Singh to provide for military leadership" and "confidence of militants having been shattered by Operation Blue Star". Further it is pointed out that the militants in the temple were armed with machine guns, anti tank missiles and rocket launchers and that they strongly resisted the army's attempts to dislodge them from the shrine and appeared to have planned for a long stand-off, having arranged for water to be supplied from wells within the temple compound and had stocked food provisions that could have lasted months.

The Assassination of Indira Gandhi and subsequent Anti-Sikh Riots

On the morning of 31 October, 1984, Prime Minister Indira Gandhi was shot-dead by two Sikh security guards (Satwant Singh and Beant Singh) in New Delhi. The assassination triggered fulminant violence against Sikhs across north India.

While the ruling party, Congress (I), maintained that the violence was due to spontaneous riots, its critics have alleged that the Congress members had planned a programme against the Sikhs. Its critics alleged that State-operated national television was used by the state to incite violence against the Sikhs, in violation of the Article 20.2 of the ICCPR and the Article 7 of the UDHR. Sixteen politicians were named as organisers of the riots. Many senior Congress leader were also indicted.

Other political parties, such as the Bharatiya Janata Party (BJP) strongly condemned the riots.

Two major civil-liberties organizations issued a joint report on the anti-Sikh riots naming sixteen important politicians, thirteen police officers and one hundred and ninety-eight others, accused by survivors and eye-witnesses. In January 1985, journalist Rahul Bedi of the *Indian Express* and Smitu Kothari of the People's Union for Civil Liberties "moved the High Court of Delhi to demand a judicial inquiry programme on the strength of the documentation carried out by human rights organizations.

Declaration of Khalistan and the Rise of Militancy

On 29, April, 1986, an assembly of separatist Sikhs at the Akal Takht made a declaration of an independent state of Khalistan. These events were followed by a decade of violence and conflict in Punjab before a return to normality in the region. During the late 1980s and the early 1990s, there was a dramatic rise in radical Sikh militancy in Punjab. On October 7, 1987, Khalistan was declared an independent state and Council of Khalistan, headed by Dr. Gurmit Singh Aulakh, was formed.

The period of insurgency saw clashes of the Sikh militants with the police, as well as with the Hindu-Nirankari groups. In 1987, 32 Hindus were pulled out of a bus and shot, near Lalru in Punjab. According to Human Rights Watch "In the beginning on the 1980s, Sikh separatists in Punjab committed serious human rights abuses, including the massacre of civilians, attacks upon non-Sikhs in the state and indiscriminate bomb attacks in crowded places". While the militants enjoyed some support within the Sikh separatists in the earlier period, the support for Sikh militants gradually disappeared. The insurgency weakened the Punjab economy and led to an increase in the violence in the state. With dwindling support and an increasingly effective Indian security troops eliminating the terrorists, the Sikh militancy was effectively over by early 1990s.

There were serious charges levelled by human rights activists against Indian Security forces (Headed by KPS Gill - himself a Sikh) that thousands of suspects were killed in staged shootouts and thousands of bodies were cremated/ disposed without proper identification or post-mortem.

The pro-Khalistan organization International Human Rights Organization claims that several Sikh women were reportedly gang-raped and molested by the Punjab Police and the Indian security forces during house to house searches. It also claims that looting of the villagers' property and ransacking of the entire villages happened during his reign. Amnesty International has also alleged several cases of appearances, torture, rape and unlawful detentions by the police during Punjab insurgency, for which 75-100 police officers had been convicted by December, 2002.

In reference to research Reduced to Ashes Book by a human rights group Khushwant Singh remarked *"It is spine-chilling.... Well, Mr Gill, it is not rubbish; you and the Punjab police have quite a few awkward questions to answer"*.

"Human Rights Watch" reported that since 1984, government forces in Punjab, including the Punjab Police, Border Security Force, Central Reserve Police Force and the Indian Army, have resorted to widespread human rights violations to fight the militants, including arbitrary arrest, prolonged detention without trial, torture, disappearance and summary killing of civilians and suspected militants. Family members were frequently detained and tortured to reveal the whereabouts of relatives sought by the police.

Air India Flight 182

Air India Flight 182 was operating on the Montréal-London-Delhi-Bombay route. On 23 June, 1985, the airplane operating on the route was blown up in midair by a bomb in the coast of Ireland. In all, 329 people perished, among them 280 Canadian nationals, mostly of Indian birth or descent origin and 22 Indian nationals.

The main suspects in the bombing were the members of a Sikh separatist group called the Babbar Khalsa and other related groups who were at the time agitating for a separate Sikh state called Khalistan in Punjab, India. In September, 2007, the Canadian commission investigated reports, initially disclosed in the Indian investigative news magazine *Tehelka* that an hitherto unnamed person, Lakhbir Singh Brar Rode had masterminded the explosions.

Khalistan Millitant Outfits

1. Babbar Khalsa International (BKI)
2. Khalistan Zindabad Force (KZF)
3. International Sikh Youth Federation (ISYF)
4. Khalistan Commando Force (KCF)
5. All-India Sikh Students Federation (AISSF)
6. Bhindranwale Tigers Force of Khalistan (BTFK)
7. Khalistan Liberation Army (KLA)
8. Khalistan Liberation Front (KLF)
9. Khalistan Armed Force (KAF)
10. Dashmesh Regiment
11. Khalistan Liberation Organization (KLO)

12. Khalistan National Army (KNA)
13. Kamagata Maru Dal of Khalistan
14. Shaheed Khalsa Force
15. Khalistan Guerilla Force
16. Khalistan Security Force

After the movement for Khalistan rose, many outfits were created. The most known are Babbar Khalsa, Khalistan Commando Force, Khalistan Zindabad Force and Dal Khalsa. Most of them were crushed till/in 1993. In recent years, active groups included Babbar Khalsa, International Sikh Youth Federation, Dal Khalsa, Bhindranwale Tiger Force. A unknown group till then, the Shaheed Khalsa Force, claimed credit for the marketplace bombings in New Delhi in 1997. Furtner there is never heard or written about this group.

Rajiv-Longowal Accord

Many Sikh and Hindu groups, as well as organizations not affiliated to any religion, attempted to establish peace between the Khalistan proponents and the Government of India.

The Central Government attempted to seek a political solution to the grievances of the Sikhs through the Rajiv-Longowal Accord, which took place between the late Prime Minister Rajiv Gandhi and Harchand Singh Longowal, the then President of the Akali Dal, who was assassinated a few months later. The accord recognized the religious, territorial and economic demands of the Sikhs that were thought to be non-negotiable under Indira Gandhi's tenure. The agreement provided a basis for a return to normalcy, but it was denounced by a few Sikh militants who refused to give up demand for an independent Khalistan. Harchand Singh Longowal was later assassinated by these militants. The transfer has allegedly been delayed pending an agreement on the districts of Punjab that should be transferred to Haryana in exchange.

Present Situation

The present situation in Punjab is generally regarded as peaceful and the militant Khalistan movement weakened considerably, especially due to the recent bombings throughout India giving way to more patriotism, higher level of renewed respect between the Hindus and Sikhs and to a large extent. The Sikh community maintains its own unique identity and is socially assimilated in cosmopolitan areas. India presently has a Sikh Prime Minister Manmohan Singh, who is highly regarded by both the left and right wing sections of the political spectrum.

Some organizations claim that social divisions and problems still exist in rural areas, but the present situation remains peaceful to a large extent, though support for an independent homeland may remain strong among the separatist Sikh leaders.. The separatist movement was popular in the Sikh diaspora in Europe and North America.

ROOTS OF INSURGENCY

Punjabi Suba Movement

In the 1950s and 1960s, linguistic issues in India caused civil disorder when the Central Government declared Hindi as the national language of India. The nationwide movement of linguistic groups seeking statehood resulted in a massive reorganization of states according to linguistic boundaries in 1956. At that time, Indian Punjab had its capital in Shimla and though the vast majority of the Sikhs lived in Punjab, they still did not form a majority. But if Haryana and Himachal could be separated sikhs could have a Punjab in which they could form a majority of 60 per cent against the Hindus being 40 per cent. The Akali Dal, a Sikh dominated political party active mainly in Punjab, sought to create a Punjabi Suba. This case was presented to the States Reorganization Commission established in 1953. It is generally believed that the Hindus sensed what the Sikhs had in mind. They, supported by the Hindu newspapers from Jalandhar, exhorted Punjabi Hindus to declare Hindi as their "mother tongue" instead of Punjabi in the censuses that took place, so that the Sikhs could be deprived of the argument that they were only asking for a Punjabi-speaking Suba. The demand for adoption of Punjabi for Punjabi-speaking areas first created and later intensified the rift between Hindus and Sikhs of Punjab.

The 'Green Revolution'

When the Green Revolution came to Punjab, it transformed the landscape of the state. Punjab saw increase on prosperity because of the Green Revolution. Punjab had occupational differences between Hindus and Sikhs. Most Sikhs were farmers and lived in the rural areas of Punjab. Most Hindus, were urban based and were involved in retail trade and manufacturing.

Bhindranwale and Undermining the Akalis

The second reason was attempts made by the then Prime Minister of India, Indira Gandhi to use Bhindranwale to undermine the Akali Dal (Eternal Party), a political party. The strategy backfired because Jarnail Singh Bhindranwale started challenging Indira Gandhi and the Indian government. Bhindranwale and his followers became a source of disruption and mayhem. Bhindranwale gained a lot of support from the Sikhs, rural Sikhs especially because they felt alienated from the Indian government. Their disruptions became so bad that in 1984, Indira Gandhi had to order the Indian Army to flush out Bhindranwale and his followers who were in the Harimandir Sahib complex, Sikhism's most holy shrine, in Amritsar. The operation undertaken by the Army was codenamed Operation Bluestar. Most Sikhs militants inside the complex were killed and the Akal Takht was bombed. Bullet holes are still visible in the complex.

Repercussions of the Riots

The Anti-Sikh riots across Northern India had repercussions in Punjab. Hundreds of Hindus were killed by organized gangs of Sikh militants. Trains were attacked and people were shot after being pulled from buses. However no hindu was attacked by any common sikh in Punjab. In 1987, 32 Hindus were pulled out of the bus and shot, near Lalru in Punjab by Sikh militants. According to Human Rights Watch "In the beginning on the 1980s, Sikh separatists in Punjab committed serious human rights abuses, including the massacre of civilians, attacks upon non-Sikhs in the state and indiscriminate bomb attacks in crowded places. Indira Gandhi's son and political successor, Rajiv Gandhi, tried, unsuccessfully, to bring peace to Punjab. Successive governments, like the Janata Dal government, also tried to bring peace to Punjab but failed. Between 1987 and 1991, Punjab was placed under President's rule and was governed from Delhi. Elections were eventually held in 1992 but the voter turnout at 24% was poor. A new Congress (I) government was formed and it gave the police chief of the state K.P.S. Gill a free hand. Gill was ruthless against the insurgents and his methods severely weakened the insurgency movement. However, Gill's reign is regarded as one of the bloodiest in the history of the country, thousands of innocent Sikhs were killed in fake encounters and countless disappeared from their homes in the dark. His police force was also accused of crimes such as rape and torture of women and children according to several reports by Amnesty International and Human Rights Watch.

Militant Attacks

Almost all of the Sikh militant groups in Punjab aimed to created an independent nation called Khalistan through acts of violence directed not only at members of the police and security forces, but also specifically at Hindu and Sikh civilians. In the early 1990s, a number of militant groups tried to impose "codes of conduct" for journalists; these codes carried a death penalty for those who disobeyed. Sikhs belonging to non-orthodox minority sects were also murdered.

There were also indiscriminate attacks designed to cause extensive civilian casualties: derailing trains, exploding bombs in markets, restaurants and other civilian areas etc. Many moderate Sikh political leaders were assassinated for opposing the militants, while several others were killed as a result of militant group rivalries. The extremists also kidnapped civilians for extortion and frequently murdered them when the demands were not met. Threats were also made to the minority Hindu population so as to drive them out of Punjab. In fact, a large population of Hindus left Punjab permanently in 1980's. This also led to rise to the drift of Punjabi Hindus from Punjabi culture and language. This resulted in thousands of Hindus fleeing the state.

Allegations of Human Rights Violations during Punjab Insurgency

Amnesty International reported that, from 1983 to 1994, armed groups struggling to form an independent Sikh state were responsible for "widespread" human rights violations, killing "thousands" of civilians and taking hostages. It further reported that the police responded with a "crackdown", illegally detaining, torturing and killing "hundreds of young men".

Human Rights Watch (HRW) reports that from the 1980s Sikh separatists were guilty of serious human rights violations through "...massacre of civilians, attacks upon Hindu minorities in the state and indiscriminate bomb attacks in crowded places...". HRW also reported that the government response resulted in further serious human rights violations against "tens of thousands". HRW noted that one case currently under investigation by India's National Human Rights Commission focused on allegations that "thousands" had been killed and cremated by security forces throughout Punjab.

Abatement of Extremism

In 1999, Kuldip Nayar, writing for Rediff.com, stated in his article "It is fundamentalism again", that the Sikh "masses" had rejected terrorists. By 2001, Sikh extremism and the demand for Khalistan had all but abated. Simrat Dhillon, writing in 2007 for the Institute of Peace and Conflict Studies, noted that while a few groups continued to fight, "the movement has lost its popular support both in India and within the Diaspora community". Mark Juergensmeyer, Director, Orfalea Centre for Global & International Studies, UCSB, reported in his paper "From Bhindranwalc to Bin Laden: Understanding Religious Violence", "The movement is over," as many militants had been killed, imprisoned, or driven into hiding and because public support was gone.

Extremist Activity

1947 and Before

In 1872 Kuka Sikhs were described as an "extremist Sikh sect". As part of the Indian Independence Movement, they committed a number of acts such as attacking and killing butchers.

In 1937, Rattan Singh and other Sikhs, while being transported from Indian island Andamans, assassinated several British soldiers.

Udham Singh, of Sikh background, was described variously as a freedom fighter, an "extremist revolutionary" and a terrorist. While Udham Singh was living in the UK, he shot and killed Michael O'Dwyer in London on 1, April, 1940. O'Dwyer had been the Lieutenant Governor of the Punjab at the time of Jallianwala Bagh massacre. Udham Singh was hanged in UK on 25, June, 1940 and his ashes were returned to India in 1974.

Bhagat Singh, a Sikh by religion, was active in the Indian independence struggle. He was called an extremist by Mahatama Gandhi. He murdered a Lahore Police Officer and his mercy plea was rejected by British Viceroy of India Lord Irwin.

1980s

Immediately after Operation Blue Star, authorities were unprepared for how quickly extremism spread and gained support in Canada, with extremists "...threatening to kill thousand of Hindus by a number of means, including blowing up Air India flights."

The 1985 bombing of Air India Flight 182 off Ireland, the deadliest aircraft terror attack until the September 11, 2001 attacks and the attempted bombing of Air India Flight 301, were alleged by the Canadian government to have been carried out by Sikh extremists. However, Inderjit Singh Reyat, of the ISYF, who was found guilty of manslaughter for making the bombs, is the only individual convicted in these attacks as of 2, May, 2010.

Canadian Member of Parliament Ujjal Dosanjh, a moderate Sikh, stated that he and others who spoke out against Sikh extremism in the 1980s faced a "reign of terror".

1990s

Global Security.org. reported that, in the early 1990s, journalists who did not conform to militant-approved behaviour were targeted for death. It also reports that there were indiscriminate attacks designed to cause extensive civilian casualties: derailing trains, exploding bombs in markets, restaurants and other civilian areas between Delhi and Punjab. It further reported that militants assassinated many of those moderate Sikh leaders who opposed them and sometimes killed rivals within the militant group. It also stated that many civilians who had been kidnapped by extremists were murdered if the militants' demands were not met. Finally, it reports that Hindus left Punjab by the thousands.

In August 1991, Julio Ribeiro, then Indian Ambassador to Romania was attacked and wounded in a Bucharest assassination attempt by gunmen identified as Punjabi Sikhs.

Sikh groups claimed responsibility for the 1991 kidnapping of the Romanian chargé d'affaires in New Delhi, Liviu Radu. This appeared to be retaliation for Romanian arrests of KLF members suspected of the attempted assassination of Julio Ribeiro, then 62, the Indian Ambassador to Romania, in Bucharest. Radu was released unharmed after Sikh politicians criticized the action.

In October, 1991, *The New York Times* reported that violence had increased sharply in the months leading up to the kidnapping, with Indian security forces or Sikh militants killing 20 or more people per day and that the militants had been "gunning down" family members of police officers.

On 24, January, 1995, Tarsem Singh Purewal, editor of Britain's Punjabi-language weekly "*Des Pardes*", was killed as he was closing his office in Southall. There is speculation that the murder was related to Sikh extremism, which Purewal may have been investigating. Another theory is that he was killed in retaliation for revealing the identity of a young rape victim.

On 31 August 1995, Chief Minister Beant Singh was killed by a suicide bomber. Babbar Khalsa claimed responsibility for the assassination, but "security authorities" were reported to be doubtful of the truth of that claim. A 2006 press release by the Embassy of the United States in New Delhi indicated that the responsible organization was the Khalistan Commando Force.

On 18, November, 1998, Journalist Tara Singh Hayer, was gunned down. The publisher of the *"Indo-Canadian Times,"* a Canadian Sikh and once-vocal advocate of the armed struggle for Khalistan, he had criticized the bombing of Air India flight 182 and was to testify about a conversation he overheard concerning the bombing. Because of his murder, his 15, October, 1998, statement to police was not admissible at the trial of Ajaib Singh Bagri.

Although extremist violence had continued throughout the decade, the United States Department of State found that Sikh extremism had decreased significantly from 1992 to 1997, although the 1997 report noted that "Sikh militant cells are active internationally and extremists gather funds from overseas Sikh communities."

2000s

In 2004, violence erupted at a protest against a play, "Behzti" (Dishonour), that was to have been performed at the Birmingham Repertory Theatre. The protest organizer, Sewa Singh Mandla, Chairman of the Birmingham Council of Sikh Gurdwaras, blamed the violence on extremist members of The Sikh Federation. Amrik Singh Gill, Chairman of the Federation, said his members had taken part in the opposition to the play from the start and denied that its members played any part in the violence. Another member of the Sikh Federation, Kulwinder Singh Johal, expressed happiness that the play had been cancelled, confirmed that Sikh Federation members had taken part in the protest against the play and denied that there had been any violence on the part of the protesters. The *Sunday Herald* reported that when it appeared the play might be presented despite the protest, death threats increased and the playwright went into hiding. The play was cancelled.

In 2006, a Brooklyn, New York, jury convicted Khalid Awan of providing money and financial services to the

Khalistan Commando Force, a terrorist organization responsible for thousands of deaths in India since its founding in 1986. The investigation began in 2003, when Awan, jailed at the time for credit card fraud, bragged of his relationship with Paramjeet Singh Panjwar, leader of the KCF.

The *Indian Express* reported in its online edition on 19 June 2006 that "Police claimed" that the KZF was behind bomb blasts in Jalandhar, India, at the Inter-State Bus Terminus that left three people killed and injured 12. A police spokesman said the attack was planned by a pair of KZF leaders, one based in Pakistan and one in Canada and executed by a "local criminal".

Terry Milewski reported in a 2006 documentary for the CBC that a minority within Canada's Sikh community was gaining political influence even while publicly supporting terrorist acts in the struggle for an independent Sikh state. In response, the World Sikh Organization of Canada (WSO), a Canadian Sikh human rights group that opposes violence and extremism, sued the CBC for "defamation, slander and libel", alleging that Milewski linked it to terrorism and damaged the reputation of the WSO within the Sikh community.

Canadian journalist Kim Bolan has written extensively on Sikh extremism. Speaking at the Fraser Institute in 2007, she reported that she still received death threats over her coverage of the 1985 Air India bombing.

In February 2008, BBC Radio 4 reported that the Chief of the Punjab Police, NPS Aulakh, alleged that militant groups were receiving money from the British Sikh community. The same report included statements that although the Sikh militant groups were poorly equipped and staffed, intelligence reports and interrogations indicated that Babbar Khalsa was sending its recruits to the same terrorist training camps in Pakistan used by Al Qaeda.

A June 2008 article by Vicky Nanjappa, writing for Rediff.com, stated that a report by India's Intelligence Bureau indicated that Pakistan's Inter-Services Intelligence organization was "desperately trying to revive Sikh" militant activity in India.

In 2008, a CBC report stated that "a disturbing brand of extremist politics has surfaced" at some of the Vaisakhi parades in Canada and The Trumpet agreed with the CBC assessment. Two leading Canadian Sikh politicians refused to attend the parade in Surrey, saying it was a glorification of terrorism.

In 2008, Dr. Manmohan Singh, Prime Minister of India, expressed his concern that there might be a resurgence of Sikh extremism.

On Sunday, 24, May, 2009, armed Sikh men attacked the Gurdwara Nanaksar, the Ravidas temple in Rudolfsheim Vienna. They left 16 injured, including visiting Dera Sach Khand head Nirajnan Das, 68 and another leader, Rama Nand, 57, dead. The attack triggered protests and rioting across northern India resulting in at least one death. There were claims and denials of responsibility in the name of the Khalistan Zindabad Force and suspicions that the attack might have been made by members of a rival sect.

On 24, September, 2009, Centralchronical.com carried a report attributed to United News of India that police arrested two Babbar Khalsa "militants" earlier in the day. The article described the arrests as a "major breakthrough in the assassination case of Rulda Singh, president of the Punjab Rashtriya Sikh Sangat who was shot at and seriously injured by two unidentified persons at his residence near New Grain market on 29, July."

29, September, 2009, Rajinder Soomel was murdered on Cambie Street in Vancouver, British Columbia. The murder renewed fears of gang violence. Soomel had been released on parole shortly before his murder. In March, 2008, Soomel had been sentenced to 4 years in prison after confessing he had tried to hire an undercover police officer to kill Hardip Uppal. Uppal had identified Ravinder Soomel, younger brother of the victim, as one of 2 assassins who killed Tara Singh Hayer in 1998.

Militant Organizations

Pre-1947

Sikh involvement in militant organizations have existed Pre-1947 (before Indian Independence) and after 1947. The goal of some pre-1947 organizations being to gain Indian Independence from the British.

Ghadar Party

A militant extremist organization setup overseas to drive the British out of India. Its members were mostly from the Sikh community and were dubbed "Sikh extremists". by the British authorities at that time.

Indian National Army

The Azad Hind Fauj (Indian National Army) was formed by Mohan Singh Deb (who was described as an extremist) to free India from British rule and fought in Southeast Asia, with support from Japan, during WWII.

Post-1947

A 2007 Australian research report cited difficulties in researching both violent and non-violent activities of the various (perhaps 22, in 1987) Sikh separatist groups. Names of groups are used interchangeably in reports, intentionally or through error. Bias and sensationalism in government and media reports reduce their reliability. The illegal nature of the organizations also presents challenges. Institute for Conflict Management, on its South Asia Terrorism Portal, alleged that

Pakistan's ISI was making "serious attempts" to reinvigorate terrorism in India and that "terror groups" were working together to accomplish that goal.

Babbar Khalsa

Babbar Khalsa has been listed as a terrorist organization in the European Union, Canada, India, UK and the United States. A Canadian Sikh, Ajaib Singh Bagri, co-founder of Babbar Khalsa, said in a 1984 speech, after Hindu Mobs had murdered thousands of Sikhs in Delhi that "Until we kill 50,000 Hindus, we will not rest."

The United States has designated the Babbar Khalsa responsible for the bombing of Air India Flight 182 on 27 June 2002. According to Terry Milewski, CBC News, Canadian courts have further established that Talwinder Singh Parmar, a founder of Babbar Khalsa, was the mastermind of the Air India bombings. Milewski further reported that some parade floats portray Parmar as a "shaheed" (martyr).

Babbar Khalsa was listed in 1995 one of the 4 "major militant groups" in the Khalistan movement.

Bhindranwale Tigers Force of Khalistan

Also known variously as Bhindranwala Tigers Force of Khalistan and Bhindranwale Tiger Force, this group appears to have been formed in 1984 by Gurbachan Singh Manochahal. After the founder's death, the BTF (or BTFK) seems to have disbanded or integrated into other organizations. The BTF was listed in 1995 one of the 4 "major militant groups" in the Khalistan movement.

International Sikh Youth Federation

Lord Bassam of Brighton, then Home Office minister, stated that ISYF members working from the UK had committed "assassinations, bombings and kidnappings" and were a "threat to national security." The ISYF is listed in the UK as a "Proscribed Terrorist Group".

It was also added to the US Treasury Department terrorism list on 27 June 2002. There are allegations that the ISYF has long been supported by Pakistan's Inter-Services Intelligence organization.

Andrew Gilligan, reporting for The London Evening Standard, stated that the Sikh Federation (UK) is the "successor" of the ISYF and that its executive committee, objectives and senior members... are largely the same. The Vancouver Sun reported in February 2008 that Dabinderjit Singh was campaigning to have both the Babbar Khalsa and International Sikh Youth Federation de-listed as terrorist organizations.

It also stated of Public Safety Minister Stockwell Day that "he has not been approached by anyone lobbying to delist the banned groups". Day is also quoted as saying "The decision to list organizations such as Babbar Khalsa, Babbar Khalsa International and the International Sikh Youth Federation as terrorist entities under the Criminal Code is intended to protect Canada and Canadians from terrorism"

●●

9
Insurgency in Northeast India and Naxalite Movement

Various groups are involved in the Insurgency in Northeast India, India's north-east states, which are connected to the rest of India by a narrow strip of land known as the Siliguri Corridor or Chicken's Neck. Much of the region is notably ethnically and linguistically different from the rest of India. In the region several armed factions operate. Some groups call for a separate state, others for autonomy while some extreme groups demand nothing but complete independence.

Northeastern India consists 7 states (also known as *the seven sisters*): Assam, Meghalaya, Tripura, Arunachal Pradesh, Mizoram, Manipur and Nagaland. Tensions exist between these states and the central government as well as amongst the tribal people, who are natives of these states and migrant peoples from other parts of India.

The states have accused New Delhi of ignoring the issues concerning them. It is this feeling which has led the natives of these states to seek greater participation in self-governance. There are existing territorial disputes between Manipur and Nagaland.

There is a rise of insurgent activities and regional movements in the northeast, especially in the states of Assam, Nagaland, Mizoram and Tripura. Most of these organizations demand independent state status or increased regional autonomy and sovereignty.

Regional tensions have eased off as of late, with Indian and state governments' concerted effort to raise the living standards of the people in these regions. However, militancy still exists within the region. Among the rebellions in the area are Tripura Rebellion and Assam Conflict.

Assam

Assam has been the hotbed of militancy for a number of years due to its porous borders with Bangladesh and Bhutan. The main causes of the friction include the anti-foreigner agitation in the 1980s and the simmering Assam-Bodo tensions. The insurgency status in Assam is classified as Very Active.

ULFA

The United Liberation Front of Asom was formed in April 1979 to establish a sovereign state of Assam through an armed struggle. In recent times the organization has lost out its middle rung leaders after most of them were arrested.

NDFB

The National Democratic Front of Bodoland was formed in 1989 as the Bodo Security Force, aims to set up an autonomous region Bodoland.

Manipur

Insurgent groups in Manipur are also classified as Very Active and stem largely from the delay in statehood.

Peoples Liberation Army

The Peoples Liberation Army is a leftist organization formed in 1978 with the aim of liberating Manipur from India.

UNLF

The United National Liberation Front was created in 1964 and demands an independent socialist state of Manipur.

PREPAK

People's Revolutionary Party of Kangleipak is an armed insurgent group in Manipur demanding a separate and independent homeland.

Nagaland

Nagaland was one of several princely states in India before Independence in 1947. Insurgent groups classified as Active, mainly demand full independence. The Naga National Council led by Phizo was the first group to dissent in 1947 and in 1956 they went underground.

NSCN-IM

The National Socialist Council of Nagaland was formed in 1980 to establish a Greater Nagaland, encompassing parts of Manipur, Nagaland, the north Cachar hills (Assam). The NSCN split in 1988 to form two groups namely NSCN(IM) & NSCN(K). As of now, both the groups are in ceasefire with the Indian government. However, they continue to be actively involved in illegal activities including extortion, kidnapping, inter-factional clashes, bootlegging and recruitment.

NSCN-K

The National Socialist Council of Nagaland—Khaplang is the second faction with the same aim of a Greater Nagaland and was formed in 1988.

Tripura

The insurgent groups in Tripura were emerged in the end of the 1970s, as ethnic tensions between the Bengali immigrants and the tribal native population.

National Liberation Front of Tripura

The National Liberation Front of Tripura was formed in March 1989.

All Tripura Tiger Force

The All Tripura Tiger Force was formed in 1990 with the sole aim of the expulsion of all Bengali speaking immigrants.

Meghalaya

Problems in Meghalaya arise from the divide between tribals and non tribal settlers, identity issues and growing corruption. The activity status is classified as Active.

ANVC

The Achik National Volunteer Council was formed in 1995 with the intentions of forming an Achik Land in the Garo Hills.

HNLC

The Hynniewtrep National Liberation Council aims to free the state from Garo domination and was formed in 1992.

Mizoram

Mizoram's tensions are largely due to the simmering Assamese domination and the neglect of the Mizo people. In 1986, the Mizo accord was which brought peace to the region. Insurgency status is classified as Partially Active

Hmar People's Convention-Democracy - HPC(D)

The People's Convention-Democracy was formed in 1995 to create an independent Hmar State. It is the offspring of the Hmar People's Convention(HPC), which entered into agreement with the Government of Mizoram which results in the formation of Sinlung Hills Development Council. However, of late, they have merged with other Hmar revolutionary groups in neighbouring Manipur and Assam with the aim of bringing the Hmars under one administrative unit.

BNLF

The Bru National Liberation Front was formed in 1997 to protect the rights and dignity of the Reangs. The BNLF have surrendered with 757 of their comrades to the Mizoram Government on 21 October 2006.

NAXALITE

The **Naxalites, Naxals** or **Naksalvadis** are a Maoist communist group in India, leaders of the Naxalite-Maoist insurgency.

The Naxal name comes from the village of Naxalbari in the Indian state of West Bengal where the movement originated. The Naxals are considered far-left radical communists, supportive of Maoist political sentiment and ideology. Their origin can be traced to the split in 1967 of the Communist Party of India (Marxist), leading to the formation of the Communist Party of India (Marxist–Leninist). Initially the movement had its centre in West Bengal. In later years, it spread into less developed areas of rural central and eastern India, such as Chhattisgarh, Orissa and Andhra Pradesh through the activities of underground groups like the Communist Party of India (Maoist).

As of 2009, Naxalites were active across approximately 220 districts in twenty states of India accounting for about 40 percent of India's geographical area, They are especially concentrated in an area known as the "Red Corridor", where they control 92,000 square kilometers. According to India's intelligence agency, the Research and Analysis Wing, 20,000 armed cadre Naxalites were operating in addition to 50,000 regular cadres and their growing influence prompted Indian Prime Minister Manmohan Singh to declare them to be the most serious internal threat to India's national security.

The Naxalites are opposed by virtually all other Indian political groups.. In February 2009, the Indian Central government announced its plans for broad, co-ordinated operations in all affected states (Chhattisgarh, Orissa, Andhra

Pradesh, Maharashtra, Jharkhand, Bihar, Uttar Pradesh and West Bengal), to plug all possible escape routes of Naxalites.

The term Naxalites comes from Naxalbari, a small village in West Bengal, where a section of the Communist Party of India (Marxist) (CPM) led by Charu Majumdar, Kanu Sanyal and Jangal Santhal initiated a violent uprising in 1967. On May 18, 1967, the Siliguri Kishan Sabha, of which Jangal was the president, declared their readiness to adopt armed struggle to redistribute land to the landless. The following week, a sharecropper near Naxalbari village was attacked by the landlord's men over a land dispute. On May 24, when a police team arrived to arrest the peasant leaders, they were ambushed by a group of tribals led by Jangal Santhal and a police inspector was killed in a hail of arrows. This event encouraged many Santhal tribals and other poor people to join the movement and to start attacking local landlords.

Charu Majumdar, inspired by the doctrines of Mao Zedong, provided ideological leadership for the Naxalbari movement, advocating that Indian peasants and lower class tribals overthrow the government and upper classes by force. A large number of urban elites were also attracted to the ideology, which spread through Majumdar's writings, particularly the 'Historic Eight Documents' which formed the basis of Naxalite ideology. In 1967 Naxalites organised the All India Coordination Committee of Communist Revolutionaries (AICCCR) and later broke away from CPM. Violent uprisings were organised in several parts of the country. In 1969 the AICCCR gave birth to the Communist Party of India (Marxist-Leninist) (CPI(ML)).

Practically all Naxalite groups trace their origin to the CPI(ML). A separate offshoot from the beginning was the Maoist Communist Centre, which evolved out of the *Dakshin Desh*-group. The MCC later fused with the People's War Group to form the Communist Party of India (Maoist). A third offshoot was that of the Andhra revolutionary communists, mainly represented by the UCCRI(ML), following the mass line legacy of T. Nagi Reddy, which broke with the AICCCR at an early stage.

During the 1970s the movement was fragmented into disputing factions. By 1980 it was estimated that around 30 Naxalite groups were active, with a combined membership of 30,000. A 2004 Indian home ministry estimate puts numbers at that time as "9,300 hardcore underground cadre… [holding] around 6,500 regular weapons beside a large number of unlicensed country-made arms". According to Judith Vidal-Hall (2006), "More recent figures put the strength of the movement at 15,000 and claim the guerrillas control an estimated one fifth of India's forests, as well as being active in 160 of the country's 604 administrative districts." India's Research and Analysis Wing, believed in 2006 that 20,000 Naxals were involved in the growing insurgency.

Today, some Naxalite groups have become legal organisations participating in parliamentary elections, such as the Communist Party of India (Marxist-Leninist) Liberation. Others, such as the Communist Party of India (Maoist) and the Communist Party of India (Marxist-Leninist) Janashakti, are engaged in armed guerrilla struggles.

On 6 April, 2010 Naxalites launched the biggest assault in the history of the Naxalite movement by killing 76 security personnel. The attack was launched by up to 1000 Naxalites in a well-planned attack, killing an estimated 76 CRPF policemen in two separate ambushes and wounding 50 others, in the jungles of Chattisgarh's Dantewada district. On 17th May naxals blew up a bus on Dantewda-sukhma road in Chhattisgarh, killing 15 policemen and 20 civilians. In third Major attack by Naxals on 29th June, at least 26 personnels of Indian Centre Reserve Forces (CRPF) were killed in Narayanpur district of Chhattisgarh.

Violence in Bengal

The Naxalites gained a strong presence amongst the radical sections of the student movement in Calcutta. Students left school to join the Naxalites. Majumdar, to entice more students into his organisation, declared that revolutionary warfare was to take place not only in the rural areas as before, but everywhere and spontaneously. Thus Majumdar declared an "annihilation line", a dictum that Naxalites should assassinate individual "class enemies" such as landlords, university teachers, police officers, politicians and others.

Throughout Calcutta, schools were shut down. Naxalites took over Jadavpur University and used the machine shop facilities to make pipe guns to attack the police. Their headquarters became Presidency College, Kolkata. The Naxalites found supporters among some of the educated elite and Delhi's prestigious St. Stephen's College, alma mater of many contemporary Indian leaders and thinkers, became a hotbed of Naxalite activities.

The Chief Minister, Siddhartha Shankar Ray, instituted counter-measures against the Naxalites. The West Bengal police fought back to stop the Naxalites. After suffering losses and facing the public rejection of Majumdar's "annihilation line", the Naxalites alleged human rights violations by the West Bengal police, who responded that the state was effectively fighting a civil war and that democratic pleasantries had no place in a war, especially when the opponent did not fight within the norms of democracy and civility.

Large sections of the Naxal movement began to question Majumdar's leadership. In 1971 the CPI(ML) was split, as the Satyanarayan Singh revolted against Majumdar's leadership. In 1972 Majumdar was arrested by the police and died in Alipore Jail. His death accelerated the fragmentation of the movement.

Reasons for Failure of Naxalite Movement

In a methodical study Dr. Sailen Debnath has surmised the consequences and reasons of failures of the Naxalite Movement organized by Charu Majumdar and Kanu Sanyal. He writes "The Naxalite movement, though continued intensively from 1967 to the middle of 1970s and resurfaced after some years, could not go a long way achieving anything commendable because of the following reasons:

1. The Naxalites wanted to surround the towns and cities by the villages, i.e. they wanted to encircle the urban centres with organized peasant forces of the villages. If the peasant militia could have occupied the cities, according to Majumdar, the so-called bourgeois government would fall making the passage to the coming of a socialist government; but the Naxalites could not and did not come up to a stage capable of organizing the peasants and thereby encircling the towns.

2. Majumdar gave sole importance to secret organization and armed training of its members for the purpose of eliminating the class enemies. As the Naxalites did not have mass level organization, they lacked mass support. Only with select few armed elements not properly educated in political line no big thing could be done.

3. "Khatam" or the action of eliminating the so-called class enemies in villages was a wrong principle of political mobilization by individual murder of select few people whose political class- character was never adjudged by their socio-economic conditions and the properties they possessed, but very often only by their political affiliation or by the name and colour of the party or parties they directly or indirectly belonged to for a long or a short period of time. As for example

in Jalpaiguri and Alipurduar they killed some petty jotdars who otherwise could have been comrades in action against the capitalists or could be friends in a revolution for radical change.

4. Recruitment in the Naxalite party was never done on proper judgement and scrutiny of the political characters and behaviours of the recruits. It so happened that many people only to feast on their animosities with their personal enemies got recruited in the Naxalite party only to utilize the help of the Naxalites to have their personal enemies in the neighbourhood killed on the basis of pseudo-identification of them as class enemies.

5. In many cases dreaded criminals too enrolled themselves in the Naxalite party with the objective of getting fire arms and to train themselves in the manufacture and use of fire arms. Thus very soon the party turned to be an organization of professional criminal outfits who soon deserted the party after their training period had been over or the cherished objective of owning armaments had been met or realized. Many of these criminals with fire arms soon turned to be dacoits and in many cases they informed the police all about the hidden training centres of the Naxalites and their main purpose in doing so was to have the original Naxalites arrested or else they themselves might fall victims of the Naxalites' targets as approvers in favour of the government..

6. The ruling Congress party inserted their supporters inside the unguarded and porous Naxalite organization for the purpose of knowing and finishing its secret bases and arresting its supporters and in the same way, the personnels of the government intelligence branch and police too in disguise of

Naxalite sympathizers got into the party's inner organization and rounded most of its leaders including Charu Majumdar into the jail. Thus police had information all about the movements of Majumdar after he had gone underground in 1970 and he was nabbed in Calcutta (Now Bangla Desh) in July, 1972. The end of his life came in the jail in some days after his arrest and how he had to pass through the gate of death, most probably in the night of 27th or 28th July, 1972, nobody except the police and the government could know properly, of course, it was told from the side of the government that he died of heart attack.

7. Ordinary people in villages were terrified at the brutal and gruesome ways they killed the fellow villagers vilifying them as class enemies. As for example, at Bholardabri in Alipurduar they killed Rajen Pandit who was a refugee from East Pakistan (Now Bangla Desh) and arduously was running a family of 12 dependents. By any means he was no class enemy at all. In another case they killed a person, chopped his head off the torso and hanged the head and the torso down the brunches of trees with ropes in two separate places, the horrible sights of which cast a gloom on the faces of bemoaning villagers. Certainly after that they could count no support from the villagers at all.

8. Unbridled repressive measures of the government proved to be more than capable in exterminating the Naxalites in the Districts of Northern Bengal as well as in the whole of West Bengal. Hundreds were slaughtered by the police and paramilitary forces in fake encounters, in jails and in police custody. Many perished because of third degree punishment. The suppression of the Naxalites did not mean to be a heavy task for a government whose objective was to

run things smoothly with the help of the British penal code of colonial era under the command of the bureaucrats, police and military who inherited the attitude of their predecessors under the British imperial Government".

Lalgarh Violence

In late May, 2009 in Lalgarh, West Bengal the Naxalites threw out the local police and staged attacks against the ruling communist government. The region came under assault by Maoist guerrillas. The state government initiated a major operation, with central paramilitary forces and state armed police, to retake Lalgarh in early June. Maoist leader Kishenji claimed in an interview that the mass Naxalite movement in Lalgarh in 2009 was aimed at creating a "liberated zone" against "oppression of the establishment Left and its police". He stated this had given the Naxalites a major base in West Bengal for the first time since the Naxalite uprising in the mid-1970s and that "We will have an armed movement going in Kolkata by 2011".

NAXALITE-MAOIST INSURGENCY

The **Naxalite-Maoist insurgency** is an ongoing conflict between Maoist groups, known as Naxalites or Naxals and the Indian government.

The insurgency started as a peasant rebellion in the eastern Indian village of Naxalbari in 1967 and has currently spread to a large swath in the central and eastern parts of the country referred to as the "Red Corridor". In 2006 Prime Minister Manmohan Singh called the Naxalites "The single biggest internal security challenge ever faced by our country." In 2009, he said the country was "losing the battle against Maoist rebels".

Naxalites claim to be supported by the poorest rural populations, especially Dalits and Adivasis. They have frequently targeted tribals, police and government workers in what they say is a fight for improved land rights and more jobs for neglected agricultural labourers and the poor and follow a strategy of rural rebellion similar to that of the protracted People's War against the government.

The Indian government's Home Secretary G K Pillai has said that he recognizes that there are legitimate grievances regarding local people's access to forest land and produce and the distribution of benefits from mining and hydro power developments, but claims that the Naxalites' long-term goal is to establish an Indian Marxist state. The Home Secretary stated that the government had decided to tackle the Naxalites head-on and take back much of the lost areas.

Naxalite

Naxalites are a group of far-left radical communists, supportive of Maoist political sentiment and ideology. Their origin can be traced to the splitting in 1967 of the Communist Party of India (Marxist), leading to the formation of the Communist Party of India (Marxist–Leninist). Initially the movement had its centre in West Bengal. In recent years, it has spread into less developed areas of rural central and eastern India, such as Chhattisgarh and Andhra Pradesh through the activities of underground groups like the Communist Party of India (Maoist). As of 2009, Naxalites are active across approximately 220 districts in twenty states of India accounting for about 40 percent of India's geographical area, They are especially concentrated in an area known as the "Red Corridor", where they control 92,000 square kilometers.

Region Affected

The Naxalites claim to operate in 182 districts in India, mainly in the states of Jharkhand, Bihar, Andhra Pradesh, Chhattisgarh, Madhya Pradesh, Maharashtra and West

Bengal. The area affected by Naxalism stretches from the border with Nepal to Karnataka in the South (2006). In West Bengal areas west of Howrah are affected by the insurgency. Chhattisgarh is the epicentre of the conflict (2007).

Areas governed by the elected Communist Party of India (Marxist) in India such as West Bengal, specifically those of Jangalmahal and Lalgarh, are some of the worst affected by anti-state violence by Maoist groups who cite the accumulation of unaccounted for wealth in the hands of CPI-M leaders and specific failure to counter problems they were elected to address such as caste discrimination and poverty.

There is a correlation between areas with extensive coal resources and impact of the insurgency. Naxalites conduct detailed socio economic surveys before starting operations in a target area.

In Chhattisgarh, the militia group Salwa Judum (which the BBC alleges is supported by the state government, an allegation rejected by the state) was constituted in response to Naxalite activities and has come under fire from pro-Maoist activist groups for "atrocities and abuse against women", employing child soldiers and looting and destruction of property.These allegations were rejected by a fact finding commission of the National Human Rights Commission of India (NHRC), appointed by the Supreme Court of India, who determined that the Salwa Judum was a spontaneous reaction by tribals against Maoist atrocities perpetrated against them.

In Bihar, the Ranvir Sena, a caste-supremacist paramilitary of the upper-caste landlords and proscribed terrorist organization by the Indian government, has been known to kill Dalit civilians in retaliation for Naxalite activity.

Similar paramilitary groups have emerged in Andhra Pradesh during the last decade. Some of these groups are Fear

Vikas, Green Tigers, Nalladandu, Red Tigers, Tirumala Tigers, Palnadu Tigers, Kakatiya Cobras, Narsa Cobras, Nallamalla Nallatrachu (Cobras) and Kranthi Sena. Civil liberties activists were murdered by the Nayeem gang in 1998 and 2000.. On 24 August 2005, members of the Narsi Cobras killed an individual rights activist and schoolteacher in Mahbubnagar district.

History

The Naxalite movement started when a militant section of CPI(M) led by Charu Majumdar and Kanu Sanyal attacked the police on 25 May 1967 in Naxalbari village in North Bengal after a farmer was killed over a land dispute. The same year the Naxalites organised the All India Coordination Committee of Communist Revolutionaries (AICCCR) and later broke away from CPI(M). In the 2000s there were peace talks with the state government of Andhra Pradesh.

2002

The People's War Group (PWG) intensified its attacks against politicians, police officers and land and business owners in response to a July ban imposed on the group by the Andhra Pradesh government. The government responded by tightening security, allegedly ordering attacks on suspected PWG members by state police and the "Green Tigers". Police forces continued to enjoy virtual impunity for the torture and killing of PWG rebels during police encounters. The Maoist Communist Center rebels intensified their armed campaign against Indian security forces following the killing of their leader by police in December.

2003

The conflict in Andhra Pradesh intensified as Naxalite rebel groups, in particular the PWG, continued guerrilla attacks on police and government targets while the security forces stepped up counter-insurgency efforts. An October assassination attempt on Chief Minister Naidu was consistent with the PWG's practice of targeting government officials to draw attention to their cause.

2004

Sporadic, low-intensity fighting between the PWG and government forces continued for most of the year. Attacks on police and TDP party officials, believed to be carried out by the PWG, accounted for most major incidents and deaths. A three-month cease-fire, announced in late June, led to failed negotiations between the government and the PWG. A few days into the cease-fire, an attack attributed to the PWG placed the cease-fire in jeopardy.

2005

Violent clashes between Maoist rebels and state security forces and paramilitary groups increased following the breakdown of peace talks between the PWG and the state government of Andhra Pradesh. Rebels continued to employ a wide-range of low-intensity guerrilla tactics against government institutions, officials, security forces and paramilitary groups. For the first time in recent years, Maoist rebels launched two large scale attacks against urban government targets. Fighting was reported in 12 states covering most of south, central and north India with the exception of India's northeast and northwest.

2006

Maoist attacks continued, primarily on government and police targets. Civilians were also affected in landmine attacks affecting railway cars and truck convoys. Clashes between state police and rebels also resulted in deaths of members of both parties and civilians that were caught in the crossfire. Fighting differs from state to state, depending on security and police force responses. In the state of Andhra Pradesh, security forces have been somewhat successful in maintaining control and combating Maoist rebels. The other state that is most affected, Chhattisgarh, has seen an increase in violence between Maoist rebels and villagers who are supported by the government.

2007

Fighting continued between Naxalite Maoists and government security forces throughout the year. The majority of hostilities took place in Chhattisgarh, which turned especially deadly when over 400 Naxalites attacked a Chhattisgarh police station, seizing arms and killing dozens. Civilians are now wedged between joining the Maoist insurgence or supporting the Salwa Judum and face coercion from both sides.

In November 2007 reports emerged that anti-SEZ (Special Economic Zone) movements such as the Bhoomi Uchched Pratirodh Committee in Nandigram in West Bengal, which arose after the land appropriation and human displacement following the SEZ Act of 2005, have joined forces with the Naxalites since February to keep the police out. Recently, police found weapons belonging to Maoists near Nandigram.

2008

Civilians were most affected in the ongoing fighting between Maoist rebels and government security forces. Of the 16 states touched by this conflict, Chhattisgarh and Jharkhand were the most affected. One positive note for Chhattisgarh was that fatalities, although still high, were significantly down from 2007. Similarly, Andhra Pradesh, the state with the most Maoist activity a few years ago, has improved security with a corresponding drop in fatality rates. Unfortunately, as conditions have improved in Chhattisgarh and Andhra Pradesh, the Maoist forces seem to have shifted their operations to the state of Orissa where conditions have worsened.

2009

In September 2009 India's Prime Minister Manmohan Singh admitted that the Maoists had growing appeal among a large section of Indian society, including tribal communities, the rural poor as well as sections of the intelligentsia and the youth. He added that "Dealing with left-wing extremism requires a nuanced strategy — a holistic approach. It cannot be treated simply as a law and order problem." In the first half of 2009, 56 Maoist attacks have been reported.

2010

In February 2010, 24 paramilitary personnel of the Eastern Frontier Rifles were killed in the Silda camp attack, an operation the guerillas stated was the beginning of "Operation Peace Hunt", the Maoist answer to the government "Operation Green Hunt" that was recently launched against them.

On 6 April 2010, Naxalite rebels killed 76 Indian soldiers and wounded 50 in a series of attacks on security convoys in Dantewada district in the central Indian state of Chattisgarh. The attack resulted in the biggest loss of life security forces have suffered since launching a large-scale offensive against the rebels.

On 17 May 2010, a Naxalite landmine destroyed a bus in Dantewada district, killing up to 44 people including several Special Police Officers (SPOs) and civilians.

On 28 May 2010 the derailment of a Kolkata–Mumbai night train killed at least 150 persons. Officials claim that Maoists are responsible for the sabotage which caused the disaster.

On 30th june 2010 26 CRPF personnel were killed in an ambush attack at Narayanpur district in chhatisgarh. Several others were injured.

Human Toll

The first combat deaths of the insurgency were in 1980. The highest number of incidents of violence has taken place in four worst-affected states—Chhattisgarh, Bihar, Jharkhand and Orissa—where 2,212 people lost their lives from January 2006 to August 2009. Around 1,100 people are known to have died during 2009. The number includes 600 civilians, 300 security personnel and 200 rebels.

There were more than 40,000 displaced people in 2006.

According to the Institute of Peace and Conflict studies, Naxal groups have recruited children in different capacities and exposed them to injury and death. However the same accusation has been levelled at the state-sponsored Salwa Judum anti-Maoist group and Special Police Officers (SPOs) assisting the government security forces.

●●

10
Unified Communist Party of Nepal

The Unified Communist Party of Nepal (Maoist), or UCPN(M), is a Nepalese political party which holds to the Maoist form of Communism. It was founded in 1994 and is currently led by Pushpa Kamal Dahal (more commonly known as Prachanda).

Following massive popular demonstrations and a prolonged "People's War" against the monarchy, the Communist Party of Nepal (Maoist) became the ruling party during the Nepalese Constituent Assembly election, 2008. The CPN(M) led a coalition government until May 4, 2009 when Prachanda resigned over a conflict with the Nepalese President, Ram Baran Yadav, regarding Prachanda's decision to sack the head of the Nepalese army, Rookmangud Katawal.

The Unified Communist Party of Nepal (Maoist) was previously the **Communist Party of Nepal (Maoist)**, until it formally unified with the Communist Party of Nepal (Unity Centre-Masal) in January 2009, resulting in its full, current name: the Unified Communist Party of Nepal (Maoist).

The CPN(M) was formed following a split in the Communist Party of Nepal (Unity Centre) and used the name CPN (Unity Centre) until 1995. On February 13, 1996 the party launched the "Nepalese People's War" and it gained control of some rural areas throughout Nepal before a ceasefire agreement was reached.

In 2001, the civil war escalated as the Maoists attacked the Nepalese Army for the first time. Although there were intermittent ceasefires, fighting was roughly continuous through 2005. In 2005, the CPN(M) sought a different strategy of seeking permanent peace accords while forming a pro-democratic alliance with several other mainstream political parties in opposition to the monarchical dictatorship of King Gyanendra. Following massive popular uprisings and protests (some involving over a million people each), a prolonged general strike in 2006 and several violent clashes between protesters and the Nepalese Army, the monarchy finally capitulated. The CPN(M) gained international legitimacy as they agreed to lay down arms and participate in the new electoral process. In the aftermath of the conflict, several western European powers removed the CPN(M) from their government's terrorist lists.

In early 2008, the CPN(M) won the largest voting bloc in the Nepalese Constituent Assembly. International observers, like the Carter Center, said that the election was held in a "peaceful, orderly" manner and were "satisfying" Other major political parties in Nepal such as the pro-democratic Nepali Congress Party and the Communist Party of Nepal (Unified Marxist-Leninist), however, accused the Maoists of using force and fraud to win the election.

Objectives

The Maoists announced a 'People's War' on February 13, 1996, under the slogan: "Let us march ahead on the path of struggle towards establishing the people's rule by wreaking the reactionary ruling system of state." Maoists strongly believe in the philosophy of Mao Zedong who proclaimed, "Political power grows out of the barrel of a gun." Maoists also draw inspiration from the 'Revolutionary Internationalist Movement', Peru's left wing guerrilla movement—the Sendero Luminoso (Shining Path) and from radical communist parties in different parts of the world.

The Maoists' aims in the 'People's War' are to establish a 'People's Democracy' in Nepal. The Maoists view it as an, "historical revolt against feudalism, imperialism and reformists." The catalyst for declaring the 'People's War' was the failure of the Nepalese Government to respond to a memorandum presented by its representatives to Prime Minister Sher Bahadur Deuba on February 4, 1996. The memorandum listed 40 demands related to "nationalism, democracy and livelihood". These included the abolition of royal privileges, the promulgation of a new constitution and the abrogation of the Mahakali treaty with India which regulated the distribution of water and electricity as well as the delineation of the border between the two countries.

Party in the House of Representative

An election for the Nepalese Constituent Assembly was held in Nepal on 10 April 2008 after having been postponed from earlier dates of 20 June 2007 and 22 November 2007. This assembly will draft a new constitution. Hence, this will decide, amongst other things, on federalism. The number of eligible voters was around 17.5 million. The Constituent Assembly has a term of two years. The Communist Party of Nepal (Maoist) (CPN (M)) placed first in the election with 220 out of 575 elected seats and it became the largest party in the Constituent Assembly. After months of power-sharing discussions and deliberations, CPN (M) Chairman Prachanda was elected as Prime Minister in August 2008. Today the party stands as the largest party of Nepal having owned 239 seats in the Constituent Assembly. The new constitution cannot be drafted without the active participation of the UCPN(M). Thus, the party holds an absolute power in the way to draft a new constitution for the state.

People's Power

A considerable number of retired Gurkha soldiers of the British and the Indian Army inhabit many of the areas previously controlled by the Communist Party of Nepal (Maoist) during the Nepalese Civil War and Nepalese security agencies have suspected that these former soldiers along with those retired and deserters from the Royal Nepalese Army (RNA) were involved in training the Communist Party of Nepal (Maoist) insurgents. Government estimates provided in early 2003 on the CPN-M strength indicated that there were approximately 31,500 combatants, 48,000 militia, 150,500 active cadres and 100,000 sympathizers. The main fighting and support forces consisted of ethnic groups like the Magars, Tharus, Limbus, Tamangs, Dalits, Brahmins and Chhetris, the last two also providing the political and military leadership). These communities are also an important vote-bank for the CPN(M) Among the Communist Party of Nepal (Maoist) fighters – about 60 per cent – were deployed in the mid-west and west in their strongholds. Another 10 percent were in the far west with around 10 percent in Gorkha and the rest were located in Kathmandu valley and east of it.

Having become the largest party of Nepal in the Nepalese Constituent Assembly, the UCP(M) has a large number of active members and a large back up of general people. After the Prachanda led government was sacked, the party led a year long peaceful movement raising the voice for the people's superiority, National collective government and nation's integrity. However, this could not produce a conclusive result. The party's youth organization Young Communist League, Nepal (YCL) plays an active role in mobilizing people for the movements held by the party. It was believed that almost 200000 people captured the state's capital on May 1 on the occasion of Labour Day.

People's Liberation Army, Nepal

People's Liberation Army, Nepal is the armed wing of the party. The PLA was founded in 2001, in the midst of the Nepal Civil War initiated by the Maoists in 1996. The chief commander of the PLA during the war was Prachanda (Pushpa Kamal Dahal). On September 12, 2008, Nanda Kishor Pun was appointed new chief commander of the PLA, as Prachanda had become Prime Minister of Nepal. This move was in line with a pledge issued by the CPN(M), issued prior to the 2008 Constituent Assembly election, that their members elected to the Assembly would leave their PLA positions.

Following the Comprehensive Peace Agreement, the PLA soldiers stay in cantoments. The party stands by the agreement whereby it states that PLA and the Royal Nepal Army should be integrated. Integration of the two armies is a one of the issue that is lagging behind with the downfall of the Prachanda government. The government claims the PLA to be under its supervision and chain of command. On the other hand, the party claims that the PLA is still under the party's chain of command and are ready to work for the party when it faces hard times.

Prachanda Path, a New Doctrine

In second conference of the CPN (Maoist), a post for Chairman was created for the Maoist chief Prachanda. Until then, the chief of the organization had been its general secretary. A report titled "The great leap forward: An inevitable need of history" was presented by Prachanda. This report was in serious discussion in the central committee and the top leaders of the party. Based on this report, the CPN (Maoist) adopted Prachanda Path as its ideology. After five years of armed struggle, the party realized that none of the proletarian revolutions of the past could be carried out on Nepal's context. So having analyzed the serious challenges and growing changes in the global arena and moving further ahead than Marxism, Leninism and Maoism, the party determined its own ideology, Prachanda Path.

Prachanda Path in essence is a different kind of uprising, which can be described as the fusion of a protracted people's war strategy which was adopted by Mao in China and the Russian model of armed revolution. Professor Lok Raj Baral, in his writing about Prachanda Path says that this doctrine doesn't apparently make an ideological break with Marxism and Leninism but finds that these doctrines' strategies aren't able to be replicated in Nepal as it was done in the past. Most of the Maoist leaders think that the adoption of Prachanda Path after the second national conference is what nudged the party into moving ahead with a clear vision ahead after five years of 'people's war'.

Senior Maoist leader Mohan Vaidya alias Kiran says, 'Just as Marxism was born in Germany, Leninism in Russia and Maoism in China, Prachanda Path is Nepal's identity of revolution. Just as Marxism has three facets — philosophy, political economy and scientific socialism, Prachanda Path is a combination of all three totally in Nepal's political context.' The adoption of Prachanda Path was inspired truly from the Shining Path. In fact, the bringing up of new doctrine worked out with the concept of giving a new identity to Nepal's revolution. Talking about the party's philosophy, Maoist chairman Prachanda says, 'The party considers Prachanda path as an enrichment of Marxism, Leninism and Maoism.' After the party brought forward its new doctrine, the government was trying to comprehend the new ideology, Prachanda Path. Meanwhile CPN Maoist intensified their armed operations against the security forces.

Women in the Party

Women have been prominent in the recruiting profile. Available reports indicate that one-fifth to one-third of the cadre and the combatants during the Nepalese Civil War may be women. Reportedly, every village under Communist Party of Nepal (Maoist) control had a revolutionary women's organization. According to a Jane's Intelligence Review report of October 2001, there were usually two women in each unit of 35-40 men and they were used to gather intelligence and act as couriers. Baburam Bhattarai was quoted as saying in *Spacetime* on April 18, 2003, that fifty percent of cadres at the lower level, thirty percent of soldiers and ten percent of members of central committee of the outfit were women. Durgha Pokhrel, then Chairman of National Women's Commission, who visited more than 25 Communist Party of Nepal (Maoist) controlled districts, stated on July 3, 2003, during a talk delivered at the Nepal Council of World Affairs that percentage of women cadres could be as high as forty. A women's group, the All Nepal Women's Association (Revolutionary), is alleged to be a front outfit of the CPN-M.

Children in the Party

During the Nepalese Civil War, the Communist Party of Nepal (Maoist) resorted to mass under-age recruitment, particularly of young students, usually between 12 and 16 years old. At the conclusion of the war, an estimated 12,000 Communist Party of Nepal (Maoist) soldiers were below 18 years of age and Human Rights Watch estimates that the majority of the current militia joined as minors. The United Nation Mission in Nepal (UNMIN) has verified that there were nine thousand child soldiers in Communist Party of Nepal (Maoist) cantonment training camps.

The Communist Party of Nepal (Maoist) used children as soldiers, messengers, cooks, porters and suppliers. Regardless of role, all children received rudimentary military training concerning explosives, so they would be able to recognize and avoid land mines. The current Unified Communist Party of Nepal (Maoist), however, continues to deny that any of its soldiers during the war were less than 18 years of age. They also claim that they have cared for orphans of adult soldiers killed in the war and that these children were not placed in danger.

Areas of Operation

During the Nepalese Civil War the guerrillas of the Communist Party of Nepal (Maoist) operated to varying degrees in 68 of the 75 districts that comprise Nepal. Their influence varied between moderate to very strong in these districts. In the districts of Rolpa, Rukum, Jajarkot, Salyan, Pyuthan and Kalikot in mid-western Nepal, The Governments presence was limited to the district headquarters with the rest of each district under Communist Party of Nepal (Maoist) control. The Nepalese Home Ministry had designated these districts as 'sensitive class A'. Nine districts, namely Dolakha, Ramechhap, Sindhuli, Kavrepalanchowk, Sindhupalchowk, Gorkha, Dang, Surkhet and Achham, had been classified as 'Sensitive Class B', while 17 'Sensitive Class C' districts where Khotang, Okhaldhunga, Udaypur, Makwanpur, Lalitpur, Nuwakot, Dhading, Tanahu, Lamjung, Parbat, Baglung, Gulmi, Arghakhachi, Bardiya, Dailekh, Jumla and Dolpa. The Communist Party of Nepal (Maoist) insurgency initially commenced in the three districts of Rolpa, Rukum and Jajarkot and eventually spread throughout Nepal. The Communist Party of Nepal (Maoist) had very strong bases in Western and mid-Western region and partially in the Eastern region.

End to the People's War

After waging the People's War for ten years, the CPN (Maoist) sat down for peace talks after the success of the People's Movement in 2002/03. The Twelve-Point Agreement reached between the then seven-party alliance and the Maoist rebels in Delhi created a path for peaceful agitation against the direct rule of the king and to end autocracy in Nepal. The people's war conducted by the CPN(M) created the foundation for the establishment of a republic in Nepal. It also created political consciousness among the people at the grassroots level and, to some extent, awareness of the need for national socio-economic transformation.

After the declaration of the King to reinstate the Parliament, the CPN(M) insisted that the declaration was a betrayal to the people. Instead the king should bring down his institution for his deeds. But there was no hearing from the other parties in the alliance. Maoist Chairman Prachanda appeared at the prime minister's residence, Baluwatar for the peace talk and said that he was there to establish a new kind of democracy in Nepal, but he didn't reveal details.

After the peace talks held between the CPN(M) and the Government of Nepal, the Maoist rebels were ready to put an end to the ten-year-long People's War. Signing the Comprehensive Peace Accord, Maoist Chairman Prachanda said that the People's War had come to an end and a new revolution was to be waged by the reinstated Parliament. The peace accord was signed in September 21, 2006 ending the Maoist revolution. However, Prachanda was able to provide legacy to the 19,000-member People's Liberation Army that was kept in the cantonment under the supervision of the United Nations Mission in Nepal (UNMIN).

The interim constitution of Nepal gave a constitutional position to these Maoist cadres. There was a provision for providing monthly allowance for the Maoist armies staying at the cantonment. The Maoist leaders believe that the revolution has not ended here but only the form of struggle was changed.

The Kharipati Meeting

The national conclave of the Maoist cadres held recently in Bhaktapur, Kharipati has ended up happily. Opposing chairman Prachanda's document, another senior leader Kiran produced a document contrary to it. The conclave ended up when a consensus was made to incorporate the spirit of both the documents and produce a new one. The cadres were split up into groups and then discussions were held about the documents produced. Majority groups including senior leaders

C.P.Gajurel, Hari Bhakta Kandel, Krishna Bahadur Mahara, Netra Bikram Chand supported Senior Leader Kiran's document. While Chairman Prachanda and his supporters as Baburam Bhattarai, Barsaman Pun got shocked seeing the majority in favour of Leader Kiran. Leader Kiran presented a document which claimed that a suitable time has come for popular uprising and setting up a people's republic contrary to Chairman Prachanda who produced a document stating that the party should move ahead creating a new statute in the favour of people and a tactical slogan for people's republic.

The conclave held several level of discussion where some disputes regarding the team leader had arisen. The team who supported Kiran's document had a leader who favoured Prachanda's document and vice-versa. The meeting ended up compromising both documents which will again be presented in the National Convention. The groups supporting Kiran's document blamed Prachanda's group for betraying the spirit of people's war and being more into luxury after holding the power. Chairman Prachanda is also blamed for sidelining the revolutionary leaders from important positions of the party and filing them up with those who support his steps. The conclave is most awaited after the Chunbang meeting which decided the party's slogan of 'Federal Democratic Republic'.

Linkage with Fraternal Parties

According to available information, the Maoists of Nepal have well-established linkages with Indian revolutionary communist organizations, primarily with the Communist Party of India (Maoist), currently leading a protracted "people's war" throughout the subcontinent. The first signs of contacts were reportedly registered during 1989-1990, when the two groups started collaborating in order to expand their influence. According to Indian government analysis, they began the process of laying a corridor, which is now widely referred to as the Revolutionary Corridor (RC) extending from Nepal to across six Indian States, including Bihar, Chhattisgarh, Jharkhand, Andhra Pradesh, Orissa and Madhya Pradesh. This entire area has been identified in Maoist literature as the Compact Revolutionary Zone (CRZ). The CRZ was organized by the Nepal and Indian members of the Naxalite movement, in a meeting at Siliguri in the Indian State of West Bengal during August 2001. Indian Maoists are known as Naxalites (or Naxals) in reference to a popular uprising that began decades ago centered in the village of Naxalbari.

Nepalese Maoists had sent their delegates to the March 2001 Congress of PWG held at Abuz Marh in the Bastar region of Chhattisgarh. The establishment of CRZ gave a wider space and platform for all the proscribed Nepal and Indian Naxalite organizations to strengthen their bases in both the countries.

The CPN(M) is a participating organization of the Revolutionary Internationalist Movement (RIM), a global association of revolutionary communist parties. In July 2001, ten regional Maoist groups formed the Coordination Committee of Maoist Parties and Organisation of South Asia (CCOMPOSA), in which the Nepalese Maoists, PWG, MCC, Purbo Banglar Sarbahara Party (Bangladesh), Communist Party of Ceylon (Sri Lanka) and other Indian communist parties became members. The appearance of graffiti in remote villages in Naxalite-strongholds, in Rayakal and Mallapur mandals (administrative unit) of Karimnagar district in Andhra Pradesh, hailing CCOMPOSA points the spread of the idea of a common front of revolutionary communist groups in South Asia. Moreover, the Central Committee of the Maoists, in late-January 2002, passed a resolution stating that it would work together with the PWG and the MCC in fighting the ban imposed on the latter two organisations in India, under the Prevention of Terrorism Act, 2002. A year earlier, in 2001, the Maoists had sent a senior leader named Gaurav as a fraternal delegate to attend the 9th Congress of the PWG. Reports indicate that the Maoists and the PWG have also formed the Indo-Nepal Border Region Committee to coordinate their activities in North Bihar and along the India-Nepal border.

During the people's war, the Maoists also gathered a lot of support from organizations in South Asia, which was very important in carrying out the struggle with certain pace. Having visited several districts in India, Maoist Chairman Prachanda studied the challenges of launching an armed struggle. Chairman Prachanda drafted war policies and tactics staying in India. Chairman Prachanda says, "First and foremost, there was the RIM Committee. There were important ideological and political exchanges. From the RIM committee we got the experience of the Communist Party of Peru, the two line struggle there and also the experience in Turkey, the experience in Iran and the experience in the Philippines." The CPN Maoist also participated in a South Asian Conference where they held discussions with the people's war group and Maoist communist Centre groups. The party believes in achieving a lot from this meet about conducting a people's war.

Having realized the necessity of spreading the party's message to the world, the party came up with a decision to host a website which was to spread the knowledge about Nepalese revolution. Thus, www.cpnm.org was hosted with the help of some of the fraternal Maoist organization in Europe. The CPN Maoist currently after the jump into the 'mainstream' politics played an initiative role in introducing a Maoist Communist Party in Bhutan as well. The new party in Bhutan is said to have greatly inspired from the Nepalese People's War and want to have a same practice there.

Split of Groups

In 2004, a small group split from the CPN(M) to form Janatantric Terai Mukti Morcha.Till today this group has split up into more than five groups and said to have no specific ideological destiny. The group accused the CPN(M) of not guaranteeing the autonomy of the Terai region. The name is in Nepalese which means "Terai Peoples Liberation Front" in English. The Jwala Singh faction of the Janatantrik Terai Mukti Morcha (JTMM-J) was formed by Nagendra Kumar Paswan a.k.a. Jwala Singh in August 2006 after he broke away from the Jaya Krishna Goit led JTMM. Jwala Singh is a former CPN-Maoist cadre and had joined Goit when he floated the JTMM. Later, he developed differences with Goit over the strategies to be adopted for the liberation of the Terai and establishment of an independent Terai state. In 2009, a faction under Matrika Yadav split from UCPN(M) to reorganise the previous Communist Party of Nepal (Maoist) i.e CPN(M).

Recent Activities

- June 16, 2006 - The CPN (M) signed a 12 point agreement with the Seven Party Alliance in order to further the Loktantra Andolan. Following this, a three month ceasefire was declared yet the process of 'forced donations' is alleged to be continuing.

- January 14, 2007 - The new 330-seat parliament, including 83 Maoists, was sworn-in after the cabinet approved an interim constitution.

- March 21, 2007 - 29 people were killed and more than 40 were injured in a deadly clash between the Madhesi People's Rights Forum (MPRF) and Maoist-aligned Madhesi Rashtriya Mukti Morcha (MRMM) cadres in Gaur. The clashes broke out over a meeting ground in Gaur which both sides wanted to use. The Interior Ministry ordered an investigation into the incident.

- April 1, 2007 - A new government was sworn in, with five Maoist ministers and one junior minister. The

Maoists were placed in charge of the ministries of information, local development, planning and works, forestry and women and children.

- September 18, 2007 - The CPN (Maoist) ministers resigned from the government due to the rejection of its demands, which included the declaration of a republic prior to the Constituent Assembly election then planned for November and an electoral system of proportional representation.
- December 31, 2007 - After agreements were reached providing for a partial proportional representation system and the abolition of the monarchy after the election, five Maoists were sworn in as ministers again. The Maoist ministers were: CPN(M) spokesman Krishna Bahadur Mahara as Minister of Communication and Information, Dev Gurung as Minister of Local Development, Hisila Yami as Minister of Physical Planning, Matrika Yadav as Minister for Forest and Soil Conservation and Pampha Bhusal as Minister for Women and Social Welfare. The first four had already been members of the government appointed in April.
- April 10, 2008 - The CPN (Maoist) participates in the 2008 Constituent Assembly election. The party gained around 30% of the vote, giving them 220 of the 575 elected seats (38%) and were nominated for 9 additional seats by the council of ministers, giving them a total of 229 of the 601 seats overall.

11
Pakistan and State Terrorism

Pakistan has been accused by Bangladesh, India, Afghanistan, Iran and other nations (including the United States and the United Kingdom) of its involvement in the terrorism in Kashmir, Afghanistan and other Indian cities. Satellite imagery from the FBI which imply the existence of terror camps and data produced by India's Research and Analysis Wing clearly suggest the existence of many terrorist camps in Pakistan with at least one militant admitting the help given by Pakistan in training them. Another terrorist out (only considered terrorist group by Indian Government), the JKLF has openly admitted that more than 3,000 militants from various nationalities were still being trained. Other nonpartisan resources also concur stating that Pakistan's military and Inter-Services Intelligence (ISI) both include personnel who sympathize with and help Islamic terrorists adding that "ISI has provided covert but well-documented support to terrorist groups active in Kashmir, including the al-Qaeda affiliate Jaish-e-Mohammed". Though Pakistan had previously denied involvement in the terrorist activities in Kashmir, President Asif Ali Zardari in a meeting with retired senior officials admitted that the terrorist outfits were "deliberately created and nurtured as a policy to achieve some short-term tactical objectives". Many Kashmir terrorist groups also maintain their headquarters in Pakistan-administered Kashmir, which is cited as further proof by the Indian Government. Many of the terrorist organisations are banned by the UN, but continue to operate under different names.

Even the normally reticent United Nations Organization (UNO) has also publicly increased pressure on Pakistan on its inability to control its Afghanistan border and not restricting the activities of Taliban "leaders" who have been declared by the UN as terrorists (not the taliban organisation). Both the Federal and State governments in India continue to accuse Pakistan of helping several banned terrorist organizations like ULFA in Assam. Experts believe that the ISI has also been involved in training and supplying Chechen militants.

Until Pakistan became a key ally in the War on Terrorism, the US Secretary of State included Pakistan on the *1993* list of countries which repeatedly provide support for acts of international terrorism. The recent 2006 transatlantic aircraft plot is also blamed by various sections in the media as being a handiwork of elements in the Pakistani administration. (See Pakistan's role in the plot) Press editorials from around the world have consistently and strongly condemned Pakistan's "terror exports".In fact, many consider that Pakistan has been playing both sides in the fight against terror, on the one hand helping to curtail it while secretly stoking terrorism. Even the noted Pakistani journalist, Ahmed Rashid has accused Pakistan's ISI of providing help to the Taliban, a statement echoed by many, including author Ted Galen Carpenter, who states that Pakistan has "assisted rebel forces in Kashmir even though those groups have committed terrorist acts against civilians" Author Gordon Thomas states that whilst aiding in the capture of Al Qaeda members, Pakistan "still sponsored terrorist groups in the disputed state of Kashmir, funding, training and arming them in their war on attrition against India."</ref> Journalist Stephen Schwartz notes that several terrorist and criminal groups are "backed by senior officers in the Pakistani army, the country's ISI intelligence establishment and other armed bodies of the state." According to one author, Daniel Byman, "Pakistan is probably today's most active sponsor of terrorism." Gordon Brown recently stated that seventy five percent terror plots in UK had links to Pakistan. Writing in The Australian Foreign editor Greg Sheridan commented 'following the terror massacres in Mumbai, Pakistan may now be the single biggest state sponsor of terrorism, beyond even Iran. Yet it has never been listed by the US State Department as a state sponsor of terrorism.'

Inter-Services Intelligence and Terrorism

Pakistan's intelligence agency, the ISI, has often been accused of playing a role in major terrorist attacks across the world including the September 11, 2001 attacks in the United States, terrorism in Kashmir, Mumbai Train bombings, London bombings, Indian Parliament Attack, Varnasi bombings, Hyderabad bombings and Mumbai terror attacks.The ISI is also accused of supporting Taliban forces and recruiting and training mujahideen to fight in Afghanistan and Kashmir. Based on communication intercepts US intelligence agencies concluded Pakistan's ISI was behind the attack on the Indian Embassy in Kabul on July 7, 2008, a charge that the governments of India and Afghanistan had laid previously. The Afghan President Hamid Karzai who has constantly reiterated allegations that militants operating training camps in Pakistan have used it as a launch platform to attack targets in Afghanistan urged western military allies to target extremist hideouts in neighbouring Pakistan. In response to the growing extremism from Pakistani border, the US has started bombing selected terrorist hideouts within Pakistan, as well as raiding villages in Pakistan to capture and kill suspected Al-Qaeda and Taliban members hiding in Pakistan.

Links to Islamic Terrorist Groups

Pakistan is also said to be a haven for terrorist groups like Al-Qaeda, Lashkar-e-Omar, Lashkar-e-Toiba, Sipah-e-Sahaba. Pakistan is accused of sheltering and training the Taliban in operations "which include soliciting funding for the Taliban, bankrolling Taliban operations, providing diplomatic support as the Taliban's virtual emissaries abroad, arranging training for Taliban fighters, recruiting skilled and unskilled manpower to serve in Taliban armies, planning and directing offensives, providing and facilitating shipments of ammunition and fuel and on several occasions apparently directly providing combat support," as quoted by the Human Rights Watch. In fact, the US has stated that the next attack on US could originate in Pakistan. Another militant outfit, the JKLF has openly admitted that more than 3,000 militants from various nationalities were still being trained. Other resources also concur stating that Pakistan's military and Inter-Services Intelligence (ISI) both include personnel who sympathize with and help Islamic militants adding that "ISI has provided covert but well-documented support to terrorist groups active in Kashmir, including Jaish-e-Mohammed" Pakistan has denied any involvement in the terrorist activities in Kashmir, arguing that it only provides political and moral support to the secessionist groups.

Many Kashmiri groups also maintain their headquarters in Pakistan-administered Kashmir, which is cited as further proof by the Indian Government. The normally reticent United Nations Organisation (UNO) has also publicly increased pressure on Pakistan on its inability to control its Afghanistan border and not restricting the activities of Taliban leaders who have been declared by the UN as terrorists.

Pakistan is *accused* of sheltering and training the Taliban in operations "which include soliciting funding for the Taliban, bankrolling Taliban operations, providing diplomatic support as the Taliban's virtual emissaries abroad, arranging training for Taliban fighters, recruiting skilled and unskilled manpower to serve in Taliban armies, planning and directing offensives, providing and facilitating shipments of ammunition and fuel and on several occasions apparently directly providing combat support," as quoted by the Human Rights Watch. In fact, the US has stated that the next attack on US could originate in

Pakistan. But this trend seems to have come to a halt as the Pakistan Army continues to mount massive military operations against Taliban and other militants in the country's Tribal Areas. This has resulted in the Taliban regularly attacking Pakistan Army convoys, encampments, even killing civilians that help Pakistan Army. In what was seen as a reversal of trends and failure of NATO forces in Afghanistan, 600 Taliban fighters crossed the border from Afghanistan in to Pakistan on January 11, 2009 but were made to retreat by the Pakistan Army contingent. The Islamic Republic of Pakistan has been branded frequently as a 'Haven for Terrorism', supporting Islamic terrorist organizations and is considered amongst the most dangerous nations in the world.. The country, with the second largest Muslim population in the world, harbours some of the most dangerous islamic terrorist organizations in the world, The **Lashkar-e-Toiba**, **The Jaish-e-Mohammed**, **The Harkat-ul-Mujahideen** and **The Hizbul Mujahideen** . The Pakistani intelligence agency, the ISI (Inter-Services Intelligence) is believed to be aiding these organizations in eradicating the existing of perceived enemies or those opposed to their cause, including India, Russia, China, Israel, US, UK and other NATO nations.

Terrorism in Afghanistan

U.S. intelligence officials claim that Pakistan's ISI sponsored the 2008 Indian Embassy bombing in Kabul. They say that the ISI officers who aided the attack had not been renegades, indicating that their actions might have been authorized by superiors. The attack was carried out by Jalaluddin Haqqani, who runs a network that Western intelligence services say is responsible for a campaign of violence throughout Afghanistan, including the Indian Embassy bombing and the 2008 Kabul Serena Hotel attack.

Terrorism in India

The government of Pakistan has come under fire for the alleged involvements of terrorist organizations operating from their soil in numerous bombings in India killing thousands over the last decade alone. Pakistan denies all allegations, stating that these acts are committed by non-state actors. The country has had a history of instability and military coups with General Pervez Musharraf coming to power after overthrowing Nawaf Sharif in 1999 and with Asif Zardari coming to power with the assassination of his wife Benazir Bhutto, allegedly by the Taliban and Al Qaeda, in 2008. The country also blames the US and India for inciting terrorism on their soil and supports the cause for Al Qaeda.

India alleged that the recent 2008 Mumbai attacks originated in Pakistan and that the attackers were in touch with a Pakistani colonel and other handlers in Pakistan. This lead to the UN ban on one such organization, the Jama'at-ud-Da'wah (which the Pakistani government has yet to enforce)

According to Indian sources there are about 37 training camps in Pakistan, 49 in Azad Kashmir and 22 in Afghanistan. The FBI also has produced images of camps operating in Pakistan. India claims that every year thousands of armed insurgents infiltrate into Indian-administered Kashmir and carry out attacks against Indian Security Forces and Kashmiri civilians. In June 2005, the Indian Army had foiled at least 72 infiltration attempts along the Line of Control in Kashmir. India alleges that despite the commitments made by Pervez Musharraf, Islamabad has done little to stop the training camps on its soil. According to India, most of the militants in Kashmir come from Pakistan, Afghanistan, Egypt, Yemen and Bangladesh. Not all Kashmiri separatists and militant organizations share the same ideology. Some fight in the name of religion, some are pro-Pakistan and some favour an independent Kashmir. While the vast majority of militants are Muslims, one report indicated a minority of fighter (40 to 50) are Hindu militants who have either taken up arms or provided safe cover for militants.

12
Gujarat Violence

The 2002 Gujarat violence describes the Godhra train burning and resulting communal riots between Hindus and Muslims. On 27 February 2002 at Godhra City in the state of Gujarat, the Sabarmati Express train was forcibly stopped and attacked by a large Muslim mob. As a result, 59 Hindu passengers — mostly women, children and seniors returning from the holy city of Ayodhya — were burned alive. The attack prompted retaliatory massacres against Muslims on a large scale, in which 790 Muslims and 254 Hindus were killed. 223 more people were reported missing. 523 places of worship were damaged: 298 dargahs, 205 mosques, 17 temples and 3 churches. Muslim-owned businesses suffered the bulk of the damage. 61,000 Muslims and 10,000 Hindus fled their homes. Preventive arrests of 17,947 Hindus and 3,616 Muslims were made. In total 27,901 Hindus and 7,651 Muslims were arrested. Nearly 10,000 rounds of bullets were fired by the police, killing 93 Muslims and 77 Hindus.

The nature of the events remains politically controversial in India. Some commentators have characterized the massacres of Muslims as a genocide in which the state was complicit, while some government sources have countered that the Muslim dead were victims of mere "riots" or "disturbances".

Godhra Train Burning

On 27 February 2002, 58 Hindus, including 25 women and 15 children, were burnt alive in a railway coach by a mob in the town of Godhra following an altercation between local

Muslims and activists of the Vishva Hindu Parishad (Kar Sevaks) returning by the Sabarmathi express train from Ayodhya. Initial media reports blamed the local Muslims for setting the coach on fire, in what Gujarat chief minister Narendra Modi and the VHP leader Giriraj Kishore alleged was a "pre-planned" attack. The *New Nanavati Report* states that the Attack on the "Kar Sevaks" on the train from Ayodhya was pre-planned and exonerates Chief Minister Narendra Modi. A previous report on the Godhra train burning, filed by Justice Banerjee, a more recent report filed by Justice Nanavati states that it was "pre-planned" by the mob. The Gujarat High Court ruling, as of 2006, has declared as illegal and unconstitutional, setting up of the Umesh Chandra Banerjee Committee, which had concluded the fire started by accident. Gujarat High Court quashed the conclusions of the Banerjee Committee and declared its formation as a "colourful exercise," "illegal, unconstitutional, null and void," and its argument of accidental fire "opposed to the prima facie accepted facts on record."

The Ahmedabad-based Forensic Science Laboratory (FSL), after conducting intensive tests, reported that it is impossible that inflammable liquid could have been poured from outside into the train compartment. One of the reason it gave was that the height of the window of the coach was around 7 feet from the ground at the place and in the position it was not possible to throw any inflammable fluid inside from outside the coach from any bucket because by doing this, most of the fluid was getting thrown outside. According to report, inflammable liquid was already present in the train compartment and fire started from inside.

However, in September 2008 the Godhra Commission confirmed that there was an attack by a mob. Going further, the report claims that one Hassan Lalu had thrown burning objects into the train and 140 litres of petrol had been used to set the train on fire, adding that stones were thrown at passengers to stop them from fleeing.

The bodies of those killed in the train were brought to Ahmedabad, where a procession was held, a move seen as a major provocation for the ensuing communal violence. The VHP issued a call for a state-wide strike on 28 February 2002, which was supported by the BJP.

Post-Godhra Violence

151 towns and 993 villages in fifteen to sixteen of the state's 25 districts were affected by the post-Godhra violence, which was particularly severe in about five or six districts. The violence raged largely between 28 February and 3 March and after a drop, restarted on 15 March, continuing till mid June. Northern and central Gujarat, as well as the north-eastern tribal belt which are closer to Godhra City, were the worst affected while Saurashtra and Kutch remained largely peaceful.

Attacks on Muslims

Attacks by large Hindu mobs began in the districts of Ahmedabad, Vadodara, Saberkantha and, for the first time in its history, Gandhinagar on 28 February. Violence spread to the largely rural districts of Panchmahals, Mehsana, Kheda, Junagadh, Banaskantha, Patan, Anand and Narmada the next day. Over the next two days, Bharuch and Rajkot and later Surat were hit.

The first incidents of attacks on the Muslim community started at Ahmedabad, where Hindus began throwing stones at and later burned a Muslim housing complex known as Gulburg Society and then spread elsewhere. The initial violence was believed to be instigated by unsubstantiated rumours, endorsed by a senior VHP leader, of Muslims having kidnapped three Hindu girls during the Godhra train attack.

In Ahmedabad, the *Dargah* of the Sufi saint-poet Wali Gujarati in Shahibaug and the 16th century Gumte Masjid mosque in Isanpur were destroyed. The Muhafiz Khan Masjid at Gheekanta was ransacked. Police records list 298 dargahs, 205 mosques, 17 temples and three churches as damaged in the months of March and April.

Attacks on Hindus

Attacks on Hindus by Muslim mobs in Danilimda, Modasa, Himmatnagar, Bharuch, Sindhi Market, Bhanderi Pole and other localities in the city of Ahmedabad in Gujarat were perpetrated by Muslim mobs. There was a significant loss of property. Late in March, more than one thousand Hindus in Dariyapur and Kalupur, including 550 dalits, fled their homes to stay in makeshift shelters after being attacked by Muslims mobs. According to the HRW report, over ten thousand Hindus were made homeless.

Several Hindu residential areas, including Mahajan No Vaado, a fortified enclave in Muslim dominated Jamalpur, were targeted following calls for retaliation.

In the morning the mosques began announcing that Islam was in danger, that there was poison in the milk. This was used as a code word. The milk was meant to be Muslims and poison meant Hindus. The rioting lasted between 2:15 p.m. and 5:30 p.m.

Residents were unable to go to work, fearing attacks. A Hindu temple in the area was destroyed. In Himmatnagar, a young man was killed when he went to a Muslim enclave on business.

Toll

According to an official estimate, 1044 people were killed in the violence — 790 Muslims and 254 Hindus including those killed in the Godhra train fire. Another 223 people were reported missing, 2,548 injured, 919 women widowed and 606 children orphaned.

Unofficial estimates put the death toll closer to 2000, with Muslims forming a high proportion of those killed.

When missing people were declared dead after 7 years, total deaths went up from 1044 to 1,267.

Security Failure

By the evening of 28 February, curfews were imposed in twenty seven towns and cities. By 25 March, thirty five towns were under curfew. Police records show 21,563 preventive arrests were made by the end of April (17,947 of the arrested were listed as Hindus and 3,616 as Muslims) as well as 13,989 substantive arrests (9,954 Hindus and 4,035 Muslims).

The New York Times' Celia Dugger reported that witnesses were "dismayed by the lack of intervention from local police", who often "watched the events taking place and took no action against the attacks on Muslims and their property". Human Rights Watch reported that in some cases members of the state police force led rioting mobs, "aiming and firing at every Muslim who got in the way", or instead of offering assistance "led the victims directly into the hands of their killers." Calls for assistance to the police, fire brigades and even ambulance services generally proved futile.

By the end of April, police recorded 170 people as killed in police firing, of whom 93 were Muslims and 77 were Hindus.

Hindu residents of Mahajan No Vaado, part of the Muslim dominated area of Jamalpur, told HRW that on 1 March, the police ignored phone calls and left them fend for themselves when a Muslim mob attacked. Numerous calls by Hindus throughout the riots were reportedly ignored by the police.

One thousand army troops were flown in by the evening of 1 March to restore order. Intelligence officials alleged that the deployment was deliberately delayed by the state and central governments. On 3 May, former Punjab Police chief K P S Gill was appointed as security adviser to the Chief Minister.

The Gujarat government transferred several senior police officers who had taken active measures to contain and investigate violent attacks to administrative positions.

RB Sreekumar, who served as Gujarat's intelligence chief during the riots, alleged that the state government issued "unconstitutional directives", with officials asking him to kill Muslims involved in rioting or disrupting a Hindu religious event. The Gujarat government denied the allegations, calling them "baseless" and instigated out of malice because Mr. Sreekumar was not promoted.

Defending the Modi administration in the Rajya Sabha against charges of genocide, BJP spokesman VK Malhotra said that the official toll of 254 Hindus, killed mostly in police firing, indicates how the state authorities took effective steps to curb the violence. BJP MP and journalist Balbir Punj disputed allegations of bias against Muslims by the BJP-run state government, pointing out that the majority of those arrested during and after the riots were Hindus.

An unidentified pamphlet circulated to journalists in Gujarat in 2007 labelled Modi's government as anti-Hindu for arresting Vishwa Hindu Parishad (VHP) workers and Hindu activists involved in the riots.

Role of Government and Police

The Gujarat state government was reprimanded immediately for failing to prevent the riots, but then increasingly for actively fomenting and participating in it, which was a far more serious charge. Critiques came repeatedly from the Supreme Court and the upper house of the Indian parliament unanimously passed a resolution calling for federal intervention in Gujarat; a similar censure motion in the lower house was defeated by about 100 votes.

The United States Department of State in its International Religious Freedom Report 2003 commented on the episode, based on a report by USCIRF:

> "India's National Human Rights Commission (NHRC), an official body, found evidence in the killings of premeditation by members of Hindu extremist groups; complicity by Gujarat state government officials and police inaction in the midst of attacks on Muslims. The NHRC also noted "widespread reports and allegations of well-organized persons, armed with mobile telephones and addresses, singling out certain homes and properties for death and destruction in certain districts-sometimes within view of police stations and personnel," suggesting the attacks may have been planned in advance. Christians were also victims in Gujarat and many churches were destroyed."

In April 2002, retired supreme court justices V. R. Krishna Iyer and P.B. Sawant headed a citizen's panel to investigate the riots. Their report includes testimony of the then Gujarat Bharatiya Janata Party (BJP) minister Haren Pandya (since murdered), who testified about an evening meeting convened by Narendra Modi the evening of the Godhra train burning. At this meeting, officials were instructed not to obstruct the Hindu rage following the incident. The report also highlighted a second meeting, held in Lunawada village of Panchmahal district, attended by state ministers Ashok Bhatt and Prabhatsingh Chauhan and other BJP and RSS leaders, where "detailed plans were made on the use of kerosene and petrol for arson and other methods of killing."

In 2003, A comment by G.T. Nanavati, who leads the official commission investigating the riots, that part of the evidence collected and reviewed till then did not indicate any serious lapse on the part of the government or police in Gujarat was criticized as inappropriate by aid and reconciliation activists and other jurists.

Organizations such as Human Rights Watch criticized the Indian government for failure to address the resulting humanitarian condition of people, the "overwhelming majority of them Muslim," who fled their homes for relief camps in the aftermath of the events; as well as the Gujarat state administration for engaging in a cover-up of the state's role in the massacres. Many of the investigations and prosecution of those accused of violence during the riots have been opened for reinvestigation and prosecution. The large-scale civil unrest has been generally been described as riots or inter-communal clashes.

In response to allegations of state involvement, Gujarat government spokesman, Bharat Pandya, told the BBC that the rioting was a spontaneous Hindu backlash fuelled by widespread anger against Muslims. He said "Hindus are frustrated over the role of Muslims in the on-going violence in Indian-administered Kashmir and other parts of India".

The US Ambassador at Large for International Religious Freedom, John Hanford, expressing concern over religious intolerance in Indian politics, said that while the rioters may have been aided by state and local officials, he did not believe that the BJP-led central government was involved in inciting the riots.

At the same time, about two hundred policemen lost their lives trying to control the violence in Gujarat.

Criminal Prosecutions

The Indian Supreme Court has been strongly critical of the state government's investigation and prosecution of those accused of violence during the riots, directing police to review about 2,000 of the 4,000 riot related cases that had been closed citing lack of evidence or leads. Following this direction, police identified nearly 1,600 cases for reinvestigation, arrested 640 accused and launched investigations against 40 police officers for their failures.

Human Rights Watch alleges that state and law enforcement officials harass and intimidate key witnesses, NGOs, social activists and lawyers who are fighting to seek justice for riot victims.

In its 2003 annual report, Amnesty International says, "the same police force that was accused of colluding with the attackers was put in charge of the investigations into the massacres, undermining the process of delivery of justice to the victims."

The Best Bakery murder trial received wide attention after witnesses retracted testimony in court and all accused were acquitted. The Indian Supreme Court, acting on a petition by social activist Teesta Setalvad, ordered a retrial outside Gujarat in which nine accused were found guilty in 2006. A key witness, Zaheera Sheikh, who repeatedly changed her testimony during the trials and the petition was found guilty of perjury.

After a local court dismissed the case against her assailants, Bilkis Bano approached the National Human Rights Commission and petitioned the Supreme Court seeking a retrial. The Supreme Court granted the motion, directing the Central Bureau of Investigation to take over the investigation, transferring the case out of Gujarat and directing the central government to appoint the public prosecutor. Charges were filed in a Mumbai court against nineteen people as well as six police officials and a government doctor over their role in the initial investigations. In January 2008, eleven men were sentenced to life imprisonment for the rape and murders and a policeman was convicted of falsifying evidence.

In 2005, the Vadodara fast track court acquitted 108 people accused of murdering two youths, during a mob attack on a group of displaced Muslims returning under police escort to their homes in Avdhootnagar. The court passed strictures against the police for failing to protect the people under their escort and failing to identify the attackers they had witnessed.

Nine people were convicted of killing a Hindu man and injuring another during group clashes in Danilimda, Ahmedabad on 12 April, while 25 others were acquitted.

Eight people, including a VHP leader and a member of the BJP, were convicted for the murder of seven members of a family and the rape of two minor girls in the village of Eral in Panchmahal district.

Fifty two people from Pavagadh and Dhikva villages in Panchmahal district were acquitted of rioting charges for lack of evidence.

A stringent anti-terror law, the POTA, was used by the Gujarat government to charge 131 people in connection to the Godhra train fire, but not invoked in prosecuting any of the accused in the post-Godhra riots. In 2005 the POTA Review Committee setup by central government to review the application of the law opined that the Godhra accused should not be tried under the provisions of POTA.

Public Enquiries

Shah-Nanavati Commission

On 6 March, the Gujarat government setup a commission of enquiry headed by retired High Court Judge K.G. Shah to enquire into the Godhra train burning and the subsequent violence and submit a report in three months. Following criticism from victims' organizations, activists and political parties over Shah's alleged proximity to the BJP, on 22 May, the government reconstituted the commission, appointing retired Supreme Court Justice G.T. Nanavati to lead the commission. In 2008, the Nanavati commission came out largely in favour of the Gujarat government's aspect. Nanavati's evidence hinged on the acquisition of 140 litres of petrol hours before the arrival of the train and the storage of the said petrol at the alleged key conspirator's, Razzak Kurkur, guest house. This was further corroborated by forensic evidence showing fuel was poured on the train compartment before being burnt. The alleged mastermind was said to be the cleric Maulvi Husain Haji Ibrahim Umarji and a dismissed Central Reserve Police Force officer named Nanumiyan, from Assam, who had instigated the Muslim crowds. Furthermore, two Kashmiris, Gulamnabi and Ali Mohammed, were in the same guesthouse for a fortnight prior to the event speaking about the Kashmir liberation movement.

The Communist Party of India (Marxist) and the Indian National Congress party both came out railing against the exoneration of the Gujarat government by the commission citing the timing of the report (with general elections months away) as evident of unfairness. Congress spokesperson Veerappa Moily commented at the strange absolvement of the Gujarat government for complacency for the carnage. He also said the report reinforced communal prejudices.

National Human Rights Commission

In its Proceedings of 1 April 2002, the Commission had set out its Preliminary Comments and Recommendations on the situation and sent a Confidential Report of the team of the Commission that visited Gujarat from 19–22 March 2002 to Gujarat government and Central Home Ministry. The Gujarat government in its reply did not provide its response to the Confidential report. Therefore, the Commission was compelled to release the confidential report in its entirety and observed that nothing in the reports received in response "rebuts the presumption that the Modi administration failed in its duty to protect the rights of the people of Gujarat" by not exercising its jurisdiction over non-state players that may cause or facilitate the violation of human rights.

It further observed that "the violence in the State, which was initially claimed to have been brought under control in seventy two hours, persisted in varying degree for over two months, the toll in death and destruction rising with the passage of time despite the measures reportedly taken by the State Government".

The report claims failure of intelligence, failure to take appropriate action, patterns of arrests, uneven handling of major cases and "Distorted FIRs: 'extraneous influences', issue of transparency and integrity" as key factors in the incident(s).

Banerjee Committee

In September 2004, a panel appointed by the central government and headed by former Supreme Court Judge UC Banerjee to probe the Godhra train fire concluded that the fire was accidental. Its findings were challenged by the BJP and the Gujarat inspector-general of police. In October 2006, the Gujarat High Court ruled that the panel was setup illegally, in violation of the Commissions of Inquiry Act, 1952 which prohibits the setting up of separate commissions by state and central governments to probe a matter of public importance.

Concerned Citizens Tribunal

The citizen tribunal headed by retired Supreme Court Justice Krishna Iyer collected evidence and testimony from more than 2000 riot victims, witnesses and others. In its report, the tribunal accuses the state government and chief Minister Modi of complicity in the violence. While Krishna Iyer was nominally part of this tribunal, he made it clear in the preface of the report that his involvement was very limited.

Aftermath

Opposition parties as well as three coalition partners of the BJP-led central government demanded the dismissal of Gujarat Chief Minister Narendra Modi for failing to contain the violence, with some calling for the removal of Union Home Minister L K Advani as well.

On 18 July, Chief Minister Narendra Modi asked the Governor of Gujarat to dissolve the state assembly and call fresh elections. The Indian Election Commission ruled out early elections, citing the prevailing law and order situation, a decision the Union Government unsuccessfully appealed against in the Supreme Court.

In August 2002 a plot by Lashkar-e-Toiba to assassinate Narendra Modi, Praveen Togadia and other Sangh Parivar leaders was unearthed by Indian police. The terrorists were planning to setup a base in Gujarat and were trying to lure some of the riot-hit people into taking up "so-called jihadi activities" Delhi Police Special Commissioner (Intelligence) K K Paul said.

In September 2002, at least 29 people were killed when Islamic fundamentalist gunmen engaged in the Akshardham Temple attack in the city of Gandhinagar in Gujarat. The Pakistani Inter-Services Intelligence and Islamic terrorist group Lashkar-e-Toiba were accused of supporting the terrorists.

Elections were held in December and Modi was returned to power in a landslide victory.

Emails made public by the perpetrators of a series of bombings in western India in July 2008 indicated that those attacks were "the revenge of Gujarat".

Relief Efforts

Amnesty International's annual report on India in 2003 claimed the "Gujarat government did not actively fulfil its duty to provide appropriate relief and rehabilitation to the survivors".

The state government initially offered compensation payments of 200,000 rupees to the families of those who died in the Godhra train fire and 100,000 rupees to the families of those who died in the subsequent riots, which local Muslims described as discriminatory. Subsequently, the government set the compensation amount at 150,000 rupees.

By 27 March, nearly 100,000 displaced people moved into 101 relief camps. This swelled to over 150,000 in 104 camps the next two weeks. The camps were run by community groups and NGOs, with the government committing to provide amenities and supplementary services. Drinking water, medical help, clothing and blankets were in short supply at the camps. At least another 100 camps were denied government support, according to a camp organiser. and relief supplies were prevented from reaching the camps over fears that they may be carrying arms.

Relief camp organisers alleged that the state government was coercing refugees to leave relief camps, with 25,000 people made to leave eighteen camps that were shut down. Following government assurances that camps would not be shut down, the Gujarat High Court bench ordered that camp organisers be given a supervisory role to ensure that the assurances were met.

On 23 May 2008, the Union Government announced a 320 crore rupee (US $ 80 million) relief package for the victims of the riots.

Media Coverage

Covering the first major communal riots following in the advent of satellite television to India, television news channels set a precedent by identifying the community of those involved in the violence, breaking a long-standing practice.

Critical reporting on the Gujarat government's handling of the situation helped bring about the Indian government's intervention in controlling the violence. The Gujarat government banned television news channels critical of the government's response. STAR News, Zee News, Aaj Tak, CNN and local stations were blocked.

The Editorial Guild of India rejected the charge that graphic news coverage aggravated the situation, saying that the coverage exposed the "horrors" of the riots as well as the "supine if not complicit" attitude of the state, helping propel remedial action. The team also faulted Gujarati language papers *Gujarat Samachar* and the pro-Hindutva *Sandesh* of distorted and provocative reporting.

The Godhra fire received extensive news coverage until it was overtaken by the subsequent violence and the presentation of the Union budget. Television and newspaper reports, particularly local Gujarati language media, carried graphic and at times sensationalised images and accounts of the Godhra train fire. S Gurumurthy, Arvind Lavakare and columnist Rajeev Srinivasan argue that news reports emphasized the provocative behaviour of the kar sevaks on the Sabarmathi Express in an effort to rationalise the subsequent mob attack at Godhra and displace blame from the mob on to the kar sevaks.

In 2004, the weekly newspaper *Tehelka* published a hidden camera exposé alleging that a BJP legislator Madhu Srivastava bribed Zaheera Sheikh, a witness in the Best Bakery killings trial. Srivatsava denied the allegation and an inquiry committee appointed by the Indian Supreme Court drew an "adverse inference" from the video footage, though it failed to uncover evidence that money was actually paid. In a 2007 expose, the newspaper released hidden camera footage of several members of the BJP, VHP and the Bajrang Dal admitting their role in the riots. Among those featured in the tapes was the special counsel representing the Gujarat government before the Nanavati-Shah Commission, Arvind Pandya, who resigned from his post after they were made public. While the report was criticised by some as being politically motivated, some newspapers said the revelations simply reinforced what was common knowledge. The Gujarat government blocked telecast of cable news channels broadcasting the expose, a move strongly condemned by the Editors Guild of India..

The riots were also the subject of a 2004 documentary film by Rakesh Sharma (filmmaker), called Final Solution (Gujarat Riots). The film was denied entry to Mumbai International Film Festival in 2004 due to objections by Censor Board of India, but won two awards at the 54th Berlin International Film Festival (2004).

Controversies on the Riots

Atrocities Against Women

An international fact finding committee formed of experts from US, UK, France, Germany and Sri Lanka reported, "sexual violence was being used as a strategy for terrorizing women belonging to minority community in the state."

Taking a stand decried by the media and other rights groups, Nafisa Hussain, a member of the National Commission for Women accused organizations and the media of needlessly exaggerating the plight of women victims of the riots. which was strongly disputed as Gujarat did not have a State Commission for Women to act on the ground. The newspaper *Tribune* reported that "The National Commission for Women has reluctantly agreed to the complicity of Gujarat Government in the communal violence in the state." The tone of their most recent report was reported by the *Tribune* as "lenient".

Riot Cases Controversy

In April 2009, the Special Investigation Team (SIT) setup by the Supreme Court of India to investigate and expedite the Gujarat riot cases submitted before the Court that Teesta Setalvad had cooked up cases of violence to spice up the incidents. The SIT which is headed by former CBI director, R K Raghavan has said that false witnesses were tutored to give evidence about imaginary incidents by Teesta Setalvad and other NGOs. The SIT charged her of "cooking up macabre tales of killings".

The court was told that 22 witnesses, who had submitted identical affidavits before various courts relating to riot incidents, were questioned by SIT and it was found that the witnesses had not actually witnessed the incidents and they were tutored and the affidavits were handed over to them by Setalvad.

The report which was brought to the notice of the bench consisting of Justices Arijit Pasayat, P Sathasivam and Aftab Alam, noted that the much publicised case of a pregnant Muslim woman Kausar Banu being gangraped by a mob and foetus being removed from sharp weapons, was also cooked up and false.

●●

13

Anti-Christian Violence in India

Anti-Christian violence in India refers to religiously-motivated violence against Christians in India, usually perpetrated by Hindu nationalists.The acts of violence include arson of churches, re-conversion of Christians to Hinduism by force and threats of physical violence, distribution of threatening literature, burning of Bibles, raping of nuns, murder of Christian priests and destruction of Christian schools, colleges and cemeteries. According to some, the number of incidents of anti-Christian violence has multiplied since the Hindu nationalist Bharatiya Janata Party (BJP) began its rule in March 1998.

A rationale offered for violence against Christians in India is that the community is growing at an alarming rate through forced conversions. It is frequently alleged that Christian Missionaries malign Hinduism, offer beef (cow beef is illegal in India), convert poor lower caste and tribal Hindus on economic and social basis; by luring them with money, cycles, jobs, claiming magic heals and even false stories, like Jesus was Krishna's friend, and the latter sent him to spread new religion. It is also said that Partisan politics and the Hindu awakening by various Hindu organizations contribute to anti-Christian violence.

From 1964 to 1996, 38 incidents of violence against Christians were reported. In 1997, 24 such incidents were reported. Since 1998, Christians in India have faced a wave of violence. In 1998 alone, 90 incidents were reported.

The Sangh Parivar and related organizations have stated that the violence is an expression of "spontaneous anger" of "vanvasis" against "forcible conversion" activities undertaken by missionaries.

Overview

Incidents of violence against Christians have occurred in nearly all parts of India, it has largely been confined to north, central and western India, in the states of Gujarat, Maharashtra, Uttar Pradesh, Madhya Pradesh and the capital area of New Delhi – not coincidentally, while these areas have been under BJP rule.

In June 2000, four churches around India were bombed. In Andhra Pradesh, church graves were desecrated. A church in Maharashtra was ransacked. In September 2008, two churches were partly damaged in Kerala. Christian leaders described the events of September 2008 as deliberate acts by anti-socials and denied any religious motive in the attacks.

Karnataka

The 2008 wave of attacks against Christians in Karnataka includes attacks directed against Christian churches and prayer halls in Karnataka by the Bajrang Dal, with the ruling BJP government accused of involvement. The violence started from 14 September 2008 when about 20 churches were vandalized in Mangalore, Udupi, Chikkamagaluru and in other districts of Karnataka. Minor violence was later reported from the border state of Kerala. The continuing distribution of literature depicting Hindu gods in a vulgar fashion by the New Light Church, a fringe proselytizer group ignited the retaliation.

Orissa

In a well-publicised case, Graham Staines, an Australian Christian missionary was burnt to death along with his two sons Timothy (aged 9) and Philip (aged 7), while they were sleeping in his station wagon at Manoharpur village in Keonjhar district in Orissa in January 1999. He was running the Evangelical Missionary Society of Mayurbhanj, an Australian missionary society. His "distribution of beef and desecrating Hindu Deities" was the root cause of this attack. In 2003, Dara Singh was convicted of leading the gang responsible.

After Staines' murder, outbreak of violence started on 24 December 2007 at Bamunigam village of Kandhamal District. Some Hindu activists forcefully removed a Christmas decoration, put up on a site traditionally used by Hindus during Durga Puja.

In August 2008, Swami Lakshmanananda, a Hindu monk and spiritual leader, was attacked and killed. The violence that followed resulted in the death of one Christian and two Hindus. The violence later spread to 300 villages in 14 of the 30 districts in the state, resulting in 4,400 burnt houses and 50,000 homeless. Fifty-nine people were killed, while 18,000 were injured.

Gujarat

In 1997 in Gujarat, 22 churches were burnt or destroyed and another 16 damaged. Recently, there has been a sharp increase in violent attacks on Christians. A Hindu group claims to have converted 2,000 tribal Christians to Hinduism. The attackers had vandalized places of worship and thus caused strike terror among the tribals. On 18 September, the Central Government issued an advisory under Article 355 of the Constitution to the Orissa government along with Karnataka.

Politics

Vishva Hindu Parishad (VHP), Bajrang Dal and Rashtriya Swayamsevak Sangh are the most accused Hindu organizations for violence against Christians in India. Sangh Parivar and local media were involved in promoting anti-Christian propaganda in Gujarat. It is evident from the ruling BJP governments in Gujarat, Orissa and Karnataka that serious lapses in handling the violence against minorities as the police failed to solve the issue effectively and the BJP was found directly responsible for allowing bloodshed to spread.

Response

US State Department

In its annual human rights reports for 1999, the United States Department of State criticized India for "increasing societal violence against Christians." The report on anti-Christian violence listed over 90 incidents of anti-Christian violence, ranging from damage of religious property to violence against Christians pilgrims. The incidents listed in the report were attributed to local media reports and information gathered by Christian groups in India and was not independently verified.

National Commission for Minorities

In light of recent Anti-Christian violence in Karnataka by the Bajrang Dal activists, the National Commission for Minorities have said that the Karnataka government of serious lapses in handling the situation and they found directly responsible for allowing violence to spread and said the police failed to solve the issue effectively as the violence continues. They also clarified that there were no reported complaints of forced conversion registered in the state.

National Integration Council of India

On 13 October 2008, the National Integration Council of India called a special meeting chaired by Manmohan Singh,

Prime Minister of India and raised the voice against spreading anti-Christian violence in India. The Prime minister strongly condemned the violence supported by the hands of Hindu militant Hindu organizations such as Bajrang Dal, VHP etc. The Prime Minister had earlier publicly admitted that the ongoing violence against the Christian communities was a matter of great "national shame".

Pope Benedict XVI

On 12 October 2008, Pope Benedict XVI criticized the continuing Anti-Christian violence in India.

On 28 October, the Vatican called upon the memory of Mahatma Gandhi for an end to the religious violence in Orissa. In a written address to Hindus, the Vatican office said Christian and Hindu leaders needed to foster a belief in non-violence among followers. Although the Mahatma had been very strong in his opposition to conversion, he had always denounced violence as an appropriate response.

CASTE-RELATED VIOLENCE IN INDIA

Caste-related violence and hate crimes in India have occurred despite the gradual reduction of casteism in the country.

According to a report by Human Rights Watch, "Dalits and indigenous peoples (known as Scheduled Tribes or adivasis) continue to face discrimination, exclusion and acts of communal violence. Laws and policies adopted by the Indian government provide a strong basis for protection, but are not being faithfully implemented by local authorities."

Phoolan Devi

Phoolan Devi (1963 – 2001) was an Indian dacoit (bandit), who later turned politician. Born in a lower-caste *Mallaah* family, she was mistreated and abandoned by her husband. She was later kidnapped by a gang of dacoits. The upper-caste

Thakur leader of the gang tried to rape her, but she was protected by the deputy leader Vikram, who belonged to her caste. Later, an upper-caste Thakur friend of Vikram killed him, abducted Phoolan and locked her up in the Behmai village. Phoolan was raped in the village by Thakur men, until she managed to escape after three weeks.

Phoolan Devi then formed a gang of Mallahs, which carried out a series of violent robberies in north and central India, mainly targeting upper-caste people. Some say that Phoolan Devi targeted only the upper-caste people and shared the loot with the lower-caste people, but the Indian authorities insist this is a myth. Seventeen months after her escape from Behmai, Phoolan returned to the village, to take her revenge. On February 14, 1981, her gang massacred twenty-two Thakur men in the village, only two of which were involved in her kidnapping or rape. Phoolan Devi later surrendered and served eleven years in prison, after which she became a politician. During her election campaign, she was criticized by the women widowed in the Behmai massacre. Kshatriya Swabhimaan Andolan Samanvay Committee (KSASC), a Kshatriya organization, held a statewide campaign to protest against her. She was elected a Member of Parliament twice.

On July 25, 2001, Phoolan Devi was shot dead by unknown assassins. Later, a man called Sher Singh Rana confessed to the murder, saying he was avenging the deaths of 22 Kshatriyas at Behmai. Although the police were skeptical of his claims, he was arrested. Rana escaped from Tihar Jail in 2004. In 2006, KSASC decided to honour Rana for "upholding the dignity of the Thakur community" and "drying the tears of the widows of Behmai."

Andhra Pradesh

This state is considered to be one of the least caste-crime infested places of India which has not had many Dalit Massacres.

Ranvir Sena

Ranvir Sena is an caste-supremacist fringe paramilitary group based in Bihar. The group is based amongst the forward-caste landlord and carries out actions against the outlawed naxals in rural areas. It has committed violent acts against Dalits and other members of the scheduled caste community in an effort to scuttle reform movements aimed at their emancipation.

Tamil Nadu

The state of Tamil Nadu has witnessed several caste-based incidents both against Dalits and Brahmins. In 2000, three young men belonging to the Dalit undercaste were killed in the Cuddalore district of Tamil Nadu. This fuelled some localized violence in the caste-sensitive region, which has seen numerous caste-related incidents in which the majority of the victims have been Dalits. Six of the killings have been registered as murders under the Indian Penal Code and others as "Deaths under suspicious circumstances". No arrests have been made in these cases.

However, several Dalits have been arrested as *goondas* (hoodlums). The Chief Minister of Tamil-Nadu, M. Karunanidhi, has been accused of having an "anti-Dalit" bias by the radical organization "Dalit Panthers of India". Theories concerning these crimes against Dalits range from "alcohol bootleggers opposing prohibition movements among Dalits" to "inter-caste relations between an Vanniya boy and a Dalit girl". Political parties sympathetic to the Dalits have protested against these incidents and have alleged systemic biases against Dalits in several parts of the country.

Bant Singh case of Punjab

On the evening of January 5, 2006 Bant Singh, a poor Sikh Dalit, was attacked by unknown assailants. His injuries necessitated medical amputation. He alleges that this was in retaliation for actively working to secure justice for his daughter, who was gang raped by upper caste members of his village in Punjab five years earlier.

A 55-year-old Dalit Sikh woman, Sawinder Kaur has been tortured, stripped and tied to a tree in Ram Duali village of Punjab because her nephew eloped with a girl from the same community. The police arrested four persons for allegedly committing the crime on 9 September 2007.

In January, 1999 four members of the village panchayat of Bhungar Khera village in Abohar paraded a handicapped Dalit woman naked through the village. No action was taken by the police, despite local Dalit protests. It was only on July 20 that the four panchayat members were arrested, after the State Home Department was compelled to order an inquiry into the incident.

A Dalit Sikh woman, Sukhwinder Kaur of Sumel Kheri village was molested and beaten up by an octroi contractor of Malaudh when she resisted his attempt to sexually exploit her.

Kherlanji Massacre

On September 29, 2006, four members of the Bhotmange family belonging to the Dalit underclass were slaughtered in Kherlanji, a small village in Bhandara district of Maharashtra. The women of the family, Surekha and Priyanka, were paraded naked in public, then allegedly gang-raped before being murdered. Although initially ascribed by the media and by the Human Rights Watch to upper castes, the criminal act was actually carried out by Kunbi caste (classified as Other Backward Classes by Government of India) farmers for having opposed the requisition of the Dalit land to have a road built over it.

On November 23, 2006, several members of the Dalit community in the nearby district of Chandrapur staged a protest regarding this incident.The protesters allegedly turned violent and pelted stones. The police had to resort to baton charging to control the situation. Dalit leaders, however, denied that they had sparked the violence and that they were "protesting in peace".

2006 Dalit Protests in Maharashtra

In November-December 2006, the desecration of a Ambedkar statue in Kanpur (Uttar Pradesh) triggered off violent protests by Dalits in Maharashtra. Several people remarked that the protests were fueled by the Kherlanji Massacre. During the violent protests, the Dalit protesters set three trains on fire, damaged over 100 buses and clashed with police. At least four deaths and many more injuries were reported.

Later, the Kanpur Police arrested a Dalit youth Arun Kumar Balmiki for desecrating the Ambedkar statue. According to the police, the youth had "admitted to having damaged the statue in a drunken state along with two friends". Earlier in a similar case, a Dalit youth was held for desecrating an Ambedkar statue in Gulbarga, Karnataka.

In response to these protests, Raj Thackeray drew attention to another incident in Kherlanji, in which a Dalit allegedly raped a girl and killed her. Thackeray demanded action on those responsible for the rape and the subsequent death of the girl and also remarked that nobody helped the girl's family.

Rajasthan

In the Indian province of Rajasthan, between the years 1999 and 2002, crimes against Dalits average at about 5024 a year, with 46 killings and 138 cases of rape. In January 2007, a Jat girl was thrown into a canal near the border with Haryana for marrying a Dalit boy, although she swam to shore and was rescued by strangers.

Punjab

On 25 May 2009, violence and rioting broke out when thousands of protesters took to the streets in almost all major towns and cities in the Indian state of Punjab after a dalit preacher, Sant Ramanand, was attacked in a temple in Vienna, Austria. He was among 16 people injured, including another preacher Sant Nirajnan Dass and later died in hospital. Both the preachers were from a low-caste Sikh sect which has a large following in parts of Punjab and had travelled to Vienna to conduct a special service. Several high-caste Sikh groups had apparently opposed his presence and threatened violence. This happened after the preacher had reportedly made remarks about the Sikh gurus.

Other Incidents

On September 1, 2007 some Yadavs poured steaming dal on a Dalit woman and her infant daughter and beat up several other Dalits, for allowing their children to play in the premises of a temple at Shivayalay Mushari, on the outskirts of Patna.

GURJAR UNREST IN RAJASTHAN

Violence erupted in the state of Rajasthan in India on 23 May 2008 when protesters belonging to the Gujjar caste who were demanding a lower scheduled tribe status,instead of their current, higher OBC (Other Backward Class) status, lynched a policeman in Bharatpur district in Rajasthan. In response, police shot at protesters as they tried to damage railway lines and government property. At least 15 were killed on the spot.

On 24 May, the Indian army was called into help calm the violence as another 15 people were killed when police shot at a mob protesters trying to torch a police station in Sikandra.

Thousands of protesters blocked a rail route between Delhi and Mumbai. Highways had also been blocked and state authorities cancelled many buses.

Gujjars — a farming, royal, warrier and trading tribe — are classified by the government as an "Other Backward Class". They are part of the caste system that do not face as much exclusion or discrimination in society. The Gujjar community feels it has been economically and educationally left behind and it wants to be reclassified as a Scheduled Tribe. They demand scheduled tribe status so that they can qualify for government jobs and state college seats reserved solely for such groups. The Indian government has put in place an affirmative action plan that sets aside job and educational quotas for the disadvantaged groups that it classifies as Scheduled Tribes and Scheduled Castes. These tribes, the government believes, need extra assistance to overcome centuries of neglect.

The state government however has so far declined to change their status. Instead has announced to spend Rs. 2.82 billion ($ 67 million) for improving schools, clinics, roads and other infrastructure in Gujjar-dominated areas. However, Gujjar leaders have said that they "do not want money". Kirori Singh Bhainsla, the head of the main Gujjar protest organization issued a statement — "We do not accept the economic package."

Even in 2007, Gujjars in Rajasthan had fought police and members of the powerful Meena tribe that already qualifies for Scheduled Tribe benefits and is opposed to Gujjars sharing the benefits it has cornered for itself. At least 26 people were killed in that violence. In wake of the ongoing Gujjar agitation in neighbouring Rajasthan, high alert had been sounded in the border districts of Madhya Pradesh to check any spread of violence. The agitation finally ended after Rajasthan Chief Minister Vasundhara Raje agreed on a 5% reservation under a new special category.

Violence

Police in Sikandra town fired at protesters who torched a police station and two buses and shot and wounded a policeman, said Amanjit Singh Gill, Rajasthan's director-general of police. Protesters also burned down a police station in the nearby village of Chandra Guddaji, Gill said. Fifteen demonstrators died when police fired live ammunition and tear gas to halt rioting, said Singh. A police officer was also beaten to death. At least 70 injured people were hospitalized in Jaipur, the state capital and the town of Dosa.

Demonstrators blocked a major highway linking Jaipur to Agra — site of the world famous Taj Mahal monument — stranding thousands of people. Thousands of army, police and paramilitary forces patrolled villages to control the violence.

26 May witnessed sporadic violence when more than 36 towns observed a bandh to protest against the police firing. Six wagons of a goods train on its way to Agra derailed near Bandikui station in Dausa district due to tampering of rail tracks, allegedly by the Gujjars. Northern railway cancelled nine trains passing through Rajasthan and diverted several others to different routes.

Security Forces' Action

The Indian Army, the Rapid Action Force, jawans of the Rajasthan Armed Constabulary, besides the Rajasthan police, carried out patrolling in the troubled districts of Bharatpur, Karauli and Dausa as at least a dozen places, including Alwar, Kotputli and Kekri in Ajmer, Pali and Rayla in Bhilwara observed *bandhs* (closure or curtailing of city businesses, offices and civilian activity due to security fears).

Government's Response

Rajasthan Chief Minister Vasundhara Raje on 25 May said there is a limit to everything and that her government will not allow Gujjars to take the state to "ransom". "It is shocking that notorious dacoits and goonda elements, wielding arm and ammunition, have joined Kirori Singh Bainsla and are indulging in arson and violence. Such things will not be tolerated," Raje stated. The government will not allow anyone to take the state to ransom and law and order into their own hands, she warned. Raje alleged "a political party from a neighbouring state was instigating and pumping money" to fuel the violence in the state. She said the government is open for talks to resolve the issue in a peaceful manner and regretted that Bainsla has been rejecting her appeals. Expressing anguish over the violent incidents that have rocked the state since the past two days resulting in death of 37 people, Raje said there is limit for "bearing such violence and arson" and warned of stringent action against those who take the state to ransom. She said it was very unfortunate that the violence comes in the wake of the Jaipur bombings which claimed 66 lives.

On 26 February, the Chief Minister announced that she would write to the Prime Minister of India recommending placing Gujjars in the category of de-notified tribes, setting aside a reservation of 4-6 per cent for them. With post-mortem examination and the last rites yet to be performed on the bodies of 18 persons killed in police firing, the Rajasthan government on made it clear that a commando operation would be the "last option" for the recovery of the bodies now in the custody of large congregations of Gujjars at Karwadi village in Bayana tehsil of Bharatpur and at Sikandra in Dausa district. "We could have recovered the bodies in less than two hours using force. However, we will not do that considering the chances of further bloodshed," Home Minister Gulab Chand Kataria said. Parliamentary Affairs Minister Rajendra Singh Rathore told journalists here that the "Gujjar reservation is a national issue. The Cabinet has decided to write to the Prime Minister requesting him to convene a meeting of Chief Ministers to review the National Scheduled Tribe Policy document of 2006."

However, on 27 May Kirori Singh Bhainsla rejected Chief Minister Vasundhara Raje's proposal for additional reservation for the agitating community. Bainsla's rejection of the proposal was unexpected, as he had earlier welcomed Raje's move to recommend in a letter to the Prime Minister four to six percent special reservation for the community.

Political Reactions

Congress MP Sachin Pilot, after being denied permission to visit Dausa district to meet agitating Gujjar leaders. He demanded, the Rajasthan government led by Vasundhara Raje must quit as it had lost the moral right to rule after the death of 35 people in clashes, saying, "The Vasundhara Raje government has lost its moral right and constitutional authority to continue in power. It has to admit the misgivings and must quit office now. You cannot terrorise a community."

Other States

Madhya Pradesh, another state with a large Gujjar population was put on alert after the violence. Delhi was also affected for 2 days. Community members, who have decided to assemble at Gwalior in Madhya Pradesh along with the bodies of those killed in the agitation. To keep control of the situation, additional police forces have been deployed in Morena and Chambal, keeping in view large number of Gujjars residing in the region. Police were also keeping a strict vigil on the Rajghat bridge on the highway of Rajasthan border.

DALIT PROTESTS IN MAHARASHTRA

In November-December 2006, the desecration of a Ambedkar statue in Kanpur triggered off violent protests by Dalits in Maharashtra, India.

There was resentment among the Dalit in Maharashtra, due to murder of four Dalits, allegedly by a mob of Kunbis in Kherlanji village in September 2006.

On November 28, 2006, the brewing resentment in the Dalit community in Maharashtra took form of violent protests, when a statue of Dalit icon B. R. Ambedkar was desecrated by a vandal in Kanpur. Several people remarked that the protests were fueled by the Khairlanji killings, including the Maharashtra Chief Minister Vilasrao Deshmukh and the Mumbai Police Commissioner A N Roy.. Later, the Maharashtra Navnirman Sena chief Raj Thackeray claimed that the protests were stoked by certain political parties in their bid to oust Maharashtra Home Minister R. R. Patil.

Protests

On November 30, 2006 violent protests took place in several places in Maharashtra. The Dalit protestors set three trains on fire, damaged over 100 buses and clashed with police.

North Maharashtra

In Osmanabad, two persons were killed in police firing on a protesting mob. Two more deaths were reported, one each in Nanded and Nashik, during the violent protests. Subsequently, a curfew was imposed in Osmanabad, Nanded and Nandurbar towns of Maharashtra.

In Aurangabad, a crowd of 1,000 Dalit gathered to protest against desecration. Some of the protestors started pelting stones at passing vehicles, injuring six persons, including sub-inspector and a constable. The police resorted to firing in air to disperse the crowd. In Akola, a truck was set on fire on the national highway and there was heavy stone-pelting on State Transport buses.

Heavy deployment of police forces took place in affected areas. Around 1,500 people were put under preventive arrest and three persons were detained in connection with the lynching of a youth in Nashik. In Akola, the police arrested

14 persons for burning an effigy of chief minister Vilasrao Deshmukh.

Pune District

In Pune and Pimpri-Chinchwad areas, 60 vehicles were damaged and set ablaze by agitators and 13 policemen were injured. A curfew was imposed in Pimpri on November 30. On December 1, a municipal corporation bus was stoned at Bopodi chowk in Pimpri-Chinchwad.

Mumbai and its Neighbourhoods

On November 30, a mob of over 6000 protestors stopped the Deccan Queen passenger train near Ulhasnagar, asked the passengers to alight and set afire its five bogies. One compartment of a local train was set ablaze at Matunga in Mumbai. There were no injuries. Some compartments of a commuter train were also torched at Ulhasnagar and the police fired in the air to control the violent crowds. The mob in Ulhasnagar also vandalized the railway station. Suburban train services were affected in parts of Mumbai as protesters squatted on the tracks. Shops and establishments in the city were also closed in view of the protests.

Incidents of protesters setting up road blocks and pelting stones were reported in Mumbai suburbs like Kanjurmarg, Mulund, Bhandup, Trombay, Kurla, Kalina, Chembur, Kurar in Malad, Goregaon, Pali Hill in Bandra and Worli. The police reported that gangster Chhota Rajan's brother Deepak Nikhalje was responsible for violence in Chembur. Police used lathicharge and fired in the air at Kherwadi junction on the Western Express highway in Vakola, after an angry mob blocked traffic and indulged in stone pelting. In Thane, corporation-run buses were off the road due to stone pelting. A Municipal Transport Corporation bus going from Kalyan to Dombivili was set on fire at Manpada by a violent mob. Protestors also forced owners of shops and establishments to down shutters.

Over 100 buses and 35 private vehicles were damaged in stone pelting. The Mumbai Police Commissioner A N Roy put the loss at around Rs 30 lakh. BEST said 91 of its buses were damaged and four drivers and a woman passenger injured in stone pelting. At least 13 policemen, including Additional Commissioner of Police K L Bisnoi, were injured in the protests.

176 people were arrested in Mumbai. The Thane police arrested 19 persons and detained another 29.

Outside Maharashtra

The protests also spread to some parts of Maharashtra's neighbouring states, Gujarat and Karnataka. In Surat (Gujarat), a mob pelted stones and damaged vehicles. Eight persons were arrested in connection with the violence. In Hubli (Karnataka), activists belonging to various Dalit organizations stoned a dozen city buses.

Arrest of the Vandal

Many Dalit leaders, including the UP RPI vice-president S.R. Darapuri remarked that the desecration of Ambedkar statue displayed the deep-seated animosity towards Dalits in India. Janata Party president Subramanian Swamy claimed that the desecration was the work of "anti-national" elements.

However, later, the Kanpur Police arrested a Dalit youth Arun Kumar Balmiki for desecrating the Ambedkar statue. According to the police, the youth had "admitted to having damaged the statue in a drunken state along with two friends". Earlier in a similar case, a Dalit youth was held for desecrating an Ambedkar statue in Gulbarga, Karnataka.

However, some Dalits in Kanpur alleged that the youth was falsely implicated to protect the real culprits. Some Dalits protesting against Balmiki's arrest damaged vehicles and blocked traffic in Kanpur.

Meanwhile, the old descecrated statue in Kanpur was buried with full honors and quickly replaced with a new one.

Political Fallout

The Maharashtra Chief Minister Vilasrao Deshmukh requested Dalit leaders to maintain calm. The Police Commissioner of Mumbai, A N Roy, requested the state government to declare a holiday on December 6 (Dr. Ambedkar's Mahaparinirvan (Death) Day), but the Government decided against doing so. Deshmukh also called an all-party meeting. The Congress president Sonia Gandhi also pitched in to settle the issue.

Raj Thackeray accused the "anti-R.R. Patil forces" of fueling the riots. He also drew attention to another incident in Khairlanji, in which a Dalit man allegedly raped a girl and killed her. Thackeray demanded action on those responsible for the rape and the subsequent death of the girl and also remarked that nobody helped the girl's family.

In Kanpur, a Congress delegation, led by former bureaucrat P.L. Punia sat on a *dharna* (hunger strike), when the District Magistrate and the Senior Superintendent of Police prevented them from visiting the site of desecration. RPI president Ramdas Athawale also reached Kanpur to visit the site of desecration. Earlier, he had said that he will hold protests in Kanpur against the "heinous" act. However, he alleged "house arrest", after police put him under tight security in a local circuit house in Kanpur.

At the 22nd National Conference of Dalit Writers in New Delhi, the former Governor of Arunachal Pradesh, Mata Prasad declared that the agitation will continue through Dalit literature.

Ranvir Sena

Ranvir Sena is a private milita mainly based in Bihar, India. This group is thought to be formed by Bhumihar landlords. It carries out actions against Dalits and other members of the scheduled caste community as well as the Naxalites. The Ranvir Sena have been connected to many murders, rapes and thefts. It has, on several occasions, been accused of human rights abuses. It is regarded as a terrorist group and classified accordingly by the Government of India. Normally, the Ranvir Sena say themselves that they committed their crimes. The Ranvir Sena has committed violent acts against Naxalite sympathisers and other members of the militant communist party. The Bihar State government banned the Ranvir Sena in July 1995 and since then the Ranvir Sena remains proscribed.

The name *Ranvir* comes from Ranvir Baba, a supposed mythical figure and *Sena* is a Hindi word (origin: *Sanskrit sena,* meaning 'army'). As the legend goes, during the late 19th century, Ranvir Baba, a retired military man and a resident of Belaur village in Bhojpur district, protected the rights of the Bhumihars against the Rajputs. It is believed that Bhumihars asserted their power in Bhojpur because of his efforts. This gave the Ranvir Sena its name when it was founded decades later under the leadership of Brahmeshwar Singh 'Mukhiya'.

It is claimed by the Ranvir Sena, that it came into existence primarily to counter the influence of various Naxalite groups and the Communist Party of India, Marxist-Leninist (CPI-ML) Liberation in central Bihar. However the Indian government considers the group a right-wing extremist group, who serve the needs of wealthy landowners. It was founded in September 1994 in Belaur village of Udwantnagar block, Bhojpur district following the merger of private caste armies like Savarna Liberation Army and the Sunlight Sena. The forerunners to the Ranvir Sena in Bhojpur district were the Brahmarshi Sena and Kuer Sena, Kisan Morcha and Ganga Sena. These groups were smaller in size and operated with a limited area. They could not sustain for long and had withered away due to repeated Naxalite onslaughts.

Dharichan Chaudhary of Belaur founded Ranvir Sena. Its founding and continuing commander is Brahmeshwar Singh of Khopira village.

During the 1995 Bihar state elections, they killed 50 people.

They killed 10 workers in Haibaspur on the 23 March 1997. They wrote the name of the organisation in blood on the village well before they left. Most of the people Ranvir Sena killed that night belonged to families allegedly supporting Party Unity, a communist group.

They killed 16 children, 27 women and 18 men with guns on the 1st December 1997. The same night,disfigured and shot to death 5 teenage girls. Ranvir Sena said about the killings:

> "We kill children because they will grow up to become Naxalites. We kill women because they will give birth to Naxalites."

After, they killed 8 low caste people who had ferried them across the river after the attack.

On January 25, 1999, there was a massacre of 22 dalit men, women and children by Ranvir Sena in the village of Shankarbigha, Jehanabad due to their alleged Naxalite allegiance. There was another massacre two weeks later in the neighbouring village of Narayanpur, where Ranvir Sena killed twelve lower-caste people.

Membership

The core group of membership of the Ranvir Sena is formed of Brahmin Bhumihars.

Police and Politician Involvement

Some politicians are members of Ranvir Sena and some policemen have helped them on their raids. For example, in a Ranvir Sena raid in Ekwari, a village in Bihar, in April 1997, policemen opened the doors of Dalit villagers so the Ranvir Sena could go inside instead of protecting the villagers as they were supposed to. Once inside, the Sena members killed 8 Dalits. Chandradev Verma former member of Janata Dal Member of Parliament for Arrah put legalising the Ranvir Sena as one of his campaign points in the 1998 Lok Sabha elections.

Area of Operation

From Bhojpur district where it was formed, over a period of time, the Ranvir Sena spread to Jahanabad, Patna, Rohtas, Aurangabad, Gaya, Bhabhua and Buxar districts. It mobilises the landed gentry in these districts against the People's War Group (PWG), the Maoist Communist Centre (MCC) and the CPI-ML (Liberation).

Organisation

The Ranvir Sena is highly organised, has extensive influence among landowners in its areas of operation and is supposedly well-endowed with financial resources.

Ranvir Sena cadres are militarily better-organised and are better-paid than any of the private armies of the past. The cadres operate mostly underground while their leaders are believed to be living in towns.

Brahmeshwar Singh 'Mukhiya', the founder chief of the Ranvir Sena, on whose head the authorities had placed a reward of half a million Indian rupees, was the Supreme Commander of the Ranvir Sena until he was arrested in Patna on August 29, 2002 to face a large number of criminal cases, which included those related to massacres. Initial reports said that Shamsher Bahadur Singh was, on September 7, 2002, appointed new chief of the Ranvir Sena. However, according to a report of December 25, 2002, the chief of the Ranvir Sena was Bhuar Thakur until he was arrested with his two associates on December 24, 2002 near Karnol bridge on the Patna-Sasaram road in Charpokhri, Bhojpur.

Ranvir Kisan Maha Sangh is the political wing that tried to take part in the 2004 elections. The Ranvir Mahila Sangh, a women's wing, has also been created. Its members too have been trained in arms use.

Index